Axton Nexus

C++
Programming For
Multithreading With OpenMP

A Hands-On Beginner's Guide to Building High-
Performance, Concurrent Applications for
Modern Multicore Systems

Table Of Content

Disclaimer   **7**

Introduction   **10**

Part I: Foundations of Concurrent Programming   **14**

Chapter 1: Introduction to Concurrency   15

Why Concurrency Matters (Modern Multicore Systems, Performance Benefits)   15

Processes, Threads, and Parallelism   18

Concurrency vs. Parallelism   22

Challenges of Concurrent Programming (Race conditions, Data races, Deadlocks - Illustrated with code samples)   26

Practice Problems: Basic conceptual questions about processes and threads.   32

Chapter 2: C++ for Concurrency   36

C++ Basics Refresher (Variables, Data types, Functions, Control flow - Essential for beginners) 36

Pointers and Memory Management (Crucial for understanding concurrency)   42

Object-Oriented Programming in C++ (Classes, Objects, Inheritance   47

The C++ Standard Library (Containers, Algorithms - Introduction to useful components) 52

Code Samples: Examples of C++ code

demonstrating core concepts.   57

Practice Problems: C++ coding exercises to reinforce basic understanding.   61

Part II: Introducing OpenMP   **65**

Chapter 3: Getting Started with OpenMP   66

What is OpenMP? (History, Benefits)   66

Setting up Your OpenMP Environment (Compiler support, Compilation flags)   69

Your First OpenMP Program ("Hello, World!" example with detailed explanations)   72

The #pragma omp parallel Directive (Creating threads, Work-sharing)   75

Code Samples: Simple OpenMP programs with variations.   80

Practice Problems: Modifying and extending the "Hello, World!" example.   85

Chapter 4: Parallel Loops and Work-Sharing   89

The #pragma omp for Directive (Distributing loop iterations)   89

Loop Scheduling (Static, Dynamic, Guided - Explained with code)   93

Reductions (Efficiently combining results from parallel loops)   97

Common Mistakes: Race conditions in loops, Incorrect reductions.   101

Code Samples: Examples demonstrating different loop scheduling techniques and reductions.   107

Practice Problems: Parallelizing loops with varying workloads.   113

Chapter 5: Data Handling and Synchronization 117

Shared vs. Private Variables (Understanding data
scope in OpenMP) 117

Critical Sections and Atomic Operations
(Protecting shared data) 121

Synchronization Constructs (barrier, single,
master) 126

Deadlocks and How to Avoid Them (Scenarios
and solutions) 131

Code Samples: Examples showing proper and
improper data handling. 135

Practice Problems: Identifying and fixing data
races in code snippets. 141

Part III: Advanced OpenMP and Applications 147

Chapter 6: Tasks and Data Flow 148

Task-Based Parallelism with OpenMP
(Introducing the task directive) 148

Dependencies and Task Scheduling 152

Data Dependencies and depend Clause 156

Code Samples: Examples of task-based
parallelism for recursive algorithms and irregular
computations. 161

Practice Problems: Implementing parallel
algorithms using tasks. 168

Chapter 7: Memory Model and Performance
Optimization 172

The OpenMP Memory Model (Consistency,
Flushing, Data races) 172

Performance Considerations (Load balancing,

False sharing, Overhead)   176

Profiling and Tuning OpenMP Applications (Tools and techniques)   180

Best Practices: Writing efficient and scalable OpenMP code.   184

Code Samples: Optimized and unoptimized code versions with performance comparisons.   188

Practice Problems: Optimizing existing OpenMP programs.   196

Chapter 8: Real-World Applications   203

Case Study 1: Image Processing (Parallel image filtering or edge detection)   203

Case Study 2: Scientific Simulation (N-body problem, Monte Carlo methods)   208

Case Study 3: Financial Modeling (Option pricing, Portfolio optimization)   215

Project Guidelines: Outlines for more extensive projects related to each case study.   222

Chapter 9: Debugging and Troubleshooting   227

Common OpenMP Errors (Race conditions, Deadlocks, Performance issues)   227

Debugging Tools and Techniques (Debuggers with OpenMP support)   231

Tips for Writing Maintainable OpenMP Code 235

Chapter 10: Beyond the Basics   240

Advanced OpenMP Features (SIMD directives, Nested parallelism)   240

Combining OpenMP with Other Concurrency Models (e.g., MPI)   245

Future Directions of OpenMP   250

Appendices   **255**

OpenMP Directive Summary (Quick reference) 256

Glossary of Terms   260

Further Reading and Resources   266

Disclaimer

The information provided in this book is intended for educational and informational purposes only. While every effort has been made to ensure the accuracy and completeness of[1] the content, the author and publisher make no representations or warranties of any kind, express or implied, about the completeness, accuracy, reliability,[2] suitability, or availability with respect to the book or the information, products, services, or related graphics contained in the book for any purpose. Any reliance you place on such information is therefore strictly at your own risk.[3]

The code examples in this book are provided as illustrations and may require modifications to work in specific environments or with particular configurations. The author and publisher shall not be liable for any errors, omissions, or damages arising from the use of the code or the information contained in this book.

The views and opinions expressed in this book are solely those of the author and do not necessarily reflect the views or opinions[4] of the publisher. The author and publisher do not endorse any specific product, service, or company mentioned in this book.

This book is not intended to provide professional advice. For specific advice on legal, financial, or technical matters, please consult a qualified professional.

The author and publisher reserve the right to make changes to the content of this book at any time without notice.

Limitation of Liability

In no event will the author or publisher be liable for any loss or damage including without limitation, indirect or consequential loss or damage, or any[5] loss or damage whatsoever arising from loss of data or profits arising out of, or in connection with, the use of this[6] book.

External Links

This book may contain links to external websites that are not provided or maintained by the author or publisher. The author and publisher do not have any control over the content of those sites and do not guarantee the accuracy, relevance, timeliness, or completeness of any information on these external websites.

Copyright

electronic or mechanical methods, without the prior written permission of the publisher, except in the case of brief quotations embodied in critical reviews and certain other[8] noncommercial uses permitted by copyright law.[9]

By reading and using this book, you acknowledge that you have read and understood this disclaimer and agree to its terms and conditions.

Introduction

In today's world of computing, where multicore processors have become the norm, the ability to write concurrent programs is no longer a luxury, but a necessity. To extract maximum performance and efficiency from modern hardware, developers need to embrace the paradigm of parallel programming. This book, "C++ Programming for Multithreading with OpenMP: A Hands-On Beginner's Guide," serves as your comprehensive guide to embark on this exciting journey.

Whether you're a student, a hobbyist, or a professional programmer, this book will equip you with the knowledge and skills to harness the power of concurrency using C++ and OpenMP. We'll start from the ground up, assuming no prior experience with parallel programming, and gradually introduce you to the concepts, techniques, and tools needed to write high-performance concurrent applications.

Why C++ and OpenMP?

C++ remains a dominant force in high-performance computing, systems programming, and game development, offering a blend of performance, control, and expressiveness. OpenMP, a powerful API for shared-memory parallel programming, complements C++ beautifully by providing a simple and flexible way to express parallelism without the complexities of low-level thread management.

What Sets This Book Apart

This book is not just another dry theoretical text. It's a **hands-on guide** that emphasizes practical application and real-world relevance. You'll find:

- **Crystal-clear explanations:** We break down complex concepts into digestible pieces, ensuring a smooth learning curve even for complete beginners.
- **Abundant code examples:** Each concept is illustrated with clear, well-commented code examples that you can readily adapt and experiment with.
- **Engaging practice problems:** Reinforce your understanding and hone your skills with a variety of practice problems and coding exercises.
- **Real-world case studies:** Explore how OpenMP is used in real-world applications, from image processing and scientific simulations to financial modeling.
- **Focus on best practices:** Learn how to write efficient, scalable, and maintainable OpenMP code that adheres to industry standards.

A Journey of Discovery

This book will take you on a journey of discovery, starting with the fundamentals of concurrency and gradually progressing to more advanced topics. You'll learn about:

- **Processes, threads, and parallelism:** The building blocks of concurrent programming.
- **The OpenMP memory model:** How threads interact with shared memory and how to avoid data races.
- **Synchronization constructs:** Tools for coordinating the actions of threads and protecting shared data.
- **Loop scheduling and reductions:** Techniques for efficiently parallelizing loops and combining results.
- **Task-based parallelism:** Expressing parallelism in a more flexible and dynamic way.
- **Performance optimization:** Profiling and tuning your OpenMP applications for maximum speed.
- **Debugging and troubleshooting:** Identifying and resolving common errors in parallel code.

Embark on Your Parallel Programming Adventure

Whether you're aiming to accelerate your existing applications or build new ones from the ground up, this book will empower you to embrace the world of concurrency and unlock the full potential of multicore processors. Get ready to embark on an exciting adventure into the realm of parallel programming with C++ and OpenMP!

Part I: Foundations of Concurrent Programming

Chapter 1: Introduction to Concurrency

Why Concurrency Matters (Modern Multicore Systems, Performance Benefits)

In today's world, where we expect our computers to juggle countless tasks seamlessly, from browsing the web and streaming videos to running complex simulations and analyzing massive datasets, the concept of concurrency has become more critical than ever. Concurrency, in essence, is the ability of a program to execute multiple tasks seemingly at the same time.[1] But why does it matter so much?

The Rise of Multicore Systems

To understand the importance of concurrency, we need to look at how computer hardware has evolved. For many years, processors primarily relied on increasing clock speeds to boost performance. However, this approach hit a wall due to physical limitations and power consumption issues. The solution? **Multicore processors**.

Instead of a single processing unit, modern CPUs contain multiple cores, each capable of executing instructions independently.[2] This is like having multiple workers within a single machine. However, to truly harness the power of these multiple cores, software needs to be designed with concurrency in mind.

The Performance Benefits of Concurrency

Concurrency offers a range of performance advantages that are essential for modern applications:[3]

- **Increased throughput:** By dividing a task into smaller subtasks that can be executed concurrently on different cores, you can significantly increase the overall throughput and complete tasks faster.[4] Imagine a web server handling multiple user requests simultaneously instead of processing them one by one.
- **Improved responsiveness:** Concurrency allows programs to remain responsive to user input even while performing time-consuming operations in the background.[5] Think of a video editing application that lets you continue working on your project while it renders a complex effect in a separate thread.
- **Enhanced resource utilization:** Concurrency enables better utilization of system resources, such as CPU cores, memory, and I/O devices.[6] By overlapping computations with I/O operations or by keeping all cores busy, you can maximize the efficiency of your programs.[7]

- **Simplified program design:** For certain types of problems, concurrent programming can lead to more modular and easier-to-understand code. Breaking down complex tasks into independent, concurrent units can improve code organization and maintainability.[8]

Examples of Concurrency in Action

Concurrency is pervasive in modern software:

- **Web browsers:** Handle multiple tabs, downloads, and plugins concurrently.
- **Operating systems:** Manage system resources, run applications, and respond to user input concurrently.[9]
- **Games:** Render graphics, simulate physics, and process user input concurrently.[10]
- **Scientific simulations:** Perform complex calculations on large datasets concurrently.[11]
- **Financial modeling:** Analyze market data and execute trades concurrently.

The Challenges of Concurrency

While concurrency offers significant benefits, it also introduces complexities and challenges that developers need to address.[12] These challenges include:

- **Race conditions:** When multiple threads access and modify shared data simultaneously, leading to unpredictable and erroneous results.[13]
- **Deadlocks:** When two or more threads become blocked indefinitely, waiting for each other to release resources.[14]
- **Synchronization issues:** Ensuring that threads cooperate correctly and avoid data corruption.

In the following chapters, we will explore these challenges in detail and learn how to overcome them using OpenMP, a powerful tool for writing concurrent C++ programs.

Processes, Threads, and Parallelism

Now that we understand the importance of concurrency, let's dive deeper into the fundamental building blocks: **processes** and **threads**. These are the core concepts that enable programs to perform multiple tasks concurrently.

Processes: The Operating System's Perspective

A **process** is an independent, self-contained execution environment that has its own dedicated resources, such as memory space, file handles, and security privileges. Think of it as a program in action. When you launch an application, the operating system creates a process for it, allocating the necessary resources and managing its execution.

Key characteristics of processes:

- **Isolation:** Processes are isolated from each other, meaning they have their own private memory space and cannot directly access the memory of other processes. This provides stability and security, preventing one misbehaving process from crashing the entire system.
- **Resource ownership:** Each process owns its resources, ensuring that one process cannot interfere with the resources of another.
- **Heavier weight:** Processes are relatively "heavyweight" in terms of the overhead associated with creating and managing them. This is because the operating system needs to allocate significant resources and perform context switching when switching between processes.

Threads: Lightweight Units of Execution

Within a process, there can be one or more **threads**. A thread is a lightweight unit of execution that shares the same memory space and resources as its parent process. Threads are like mini-processes that operate within the confines of a larger process.

Key characteristics of threads:

- **Shared resources:** Threads within the same process share the same memory space, allowing them to communicate and cooperate efficiently. This shared memory model facilitates data sharing and reduces the overhead of inter-process communication.
- **Lighter weight:** Threads are "lightweight" compared to processes, as they require fewer resources to create and manage. Context switching between threads is also faster than switching between processes.
- **Concurrency within a process:** Threads enable concurrency within a single process, allowing multiple tasks to be executed seemingly simultaneously.

Illustrating the Relationship

To visualize the relationship between processes and threads, consider this analogy:

Imagine a large office building (the computer system). Each company occupying the building is like a **process** (e.g., a web browser, a text editor, a game). Within each company, there are multiple employees (**threads**) working on different tasks. All employees within a company share the same office space and resources (shared memory), while different companies have their own separate offices (isolated memory).

Parallelism: True Simultaneous Execution

While concurrency refers to the ability to execute multiple tasks seemingly at the same time, **parallelism** specifically refers to the simultaneous execution of multiple tasks on different processors or cores.

- **Concurrency without parallelism:** A single-core processor can achieve concurrency by rapidly switching between different threads, giving the illusion of simultaneous execution. However, true parallelism is not possible on a single core.
- **Concurrency with parallelism:** On a multicore system, threads can be executed in parallel, with each thread running on a separate core. This allows for true simultaneous execution and maximizes the utilization of available processing power.

In Summary

Processes and threads are the fundamental building blocks of concurrent programming. Understanding their characteristics and the relationship between them is crucial for writing efficient and correct concurrent programs. In the next section, we'll delve into the challenges that arise when dealing with concurrency and how to address them.

Concurrency vs. Parallelism

While the terms "concurrency" and "parallelism" are often used interchangeably, they represent distinct concepts in the world of computing.[1] It's important to understand the nuances between them to grasp the full picture of how modern software leverages multiple cores and executes tasks efficiently.

Concurrency: Managing Multiple Tasks

Concurrency is about dealing with multiple tasks at the same time.[2] It's like juggling – you might not be doing all the actions simultaneously, but you're managing multiple balls in the air. The focus is on **managing and coordinating** multiple tasks, potentially overlapping their execution.[3]

Key characteristics of concurrency:

- **Interleaving of execution:** Tasks can be executed in an interleaved manner, with the processor switching between them rapidly. This gives the illusion of simultaneous execution, even on a single-core system.
- **Focus on structure:** Concurrency is often concerned with structuring a program to handle

multiple tasks effectively, regardless of whether they are executed in parallel.[4]

- **Overlapping operations:** Concurrency can involve overlapping different types of operations, such as computation and I/O. For example, a program can read data from a file while simultaneously processing data that has already been read.

Parallelism: True Simultaneous Execution

Parallelism, on the other hand, is about doing multiple things truly at the same time. It's like having multiple workers performing different tasks simultaneously. The focus is on **increasing speed and throughput** by utilizing multiple processing units.

Key characteristics of parallelism:

- **Simultaneous execution:** Tasks are executed simultaneously on different processors or cores.
- **Focus on performance:** Parallelism aims to improve performance by dividing a task into subtasks that can be executed in parallel.[5]
- **Requires multiple cores:** Parallelism requires multiple processing units to achieve true simultaneous execution.[6]

Illustrative Examples

To further clarify the distinction, consider these examples:

- **Concurrency without parallelism:** Imagine a chef preparing a meal. They might be chopping vegetables while waiting for water to boil. This is concurrent, as the chef is managing multiple tasks, but it's not parallel, as they are only actively working on one task at a time.
- **Parallelism without concurrency (less common):** Imagine multiple chefs each dedicated to a single, specific task in preparing a meal. One chef chops vegetables, another stirs a sauce, and another prepares the main course. This is parallel, as multiple tasks are happening simultaneously, but it's not necessarily concurrent in the sense of a single entity managing multiple tasks.
- **Concurrency and parallelism:** Imagine multiple chefs working together in a coordinated manner to prepare a complex dish. One chef might be chopping vegetables, another sautéing them, and another preparing the sauce, all while coordinating their actions. This is both concurrent and parallel, as multiple tasks are being managed and executed simultaneously.

Relationship between Concurrency and Parallelism

It's important to note that parallelism is a form of concurrency, but not all concurrency is parallel.[7] Concurrency is a broader concept that encompasses various ways of managing multiple tasks, while parallelism is a specific type of concurrency that requires multiple processing units.[8]

Why the Distinction Matters

Understanding the difference between concurrency and parallelism is crucial for:

- **Designing efficient programs:** Choosing the right approach depends on the nature of the task and the available hardware.
- **Reasoning about program behavior:** Identifying potential issues like race conditions and deadlocks requires a clear understanding of how tasks are executed.
- **Utilizing hardware effectively:** Maximizing the performance benefits of multicore systems requires designing programs that can execute tasks in parallel.[9]

In the following chapters, we'll delve into the techniques and tools that enable us to write concurrent and parallel programs in C++ using OpenMP.

Challenges of Concurrent Programming (Race conditions, Data races, Deadlocks - Illustrated with code samples)

While concurrency offers significant advantages, it also introduces complexities that can lead to subtle and difficult-to-debug errors if not handled carefully. Let's explore some of the most common challenges:

1. Race Conditions

A **race condition** occurs when the behavior of a program depends on the unpredictable timing of events, such as the order in which threads execute. This can lead to unexpected and erroneous results, as the outcome of a computation may vary depending on which thread "wins the race" to access or modify shared data.

Example:

```cpp
C++

#include <iostream>
#include <thread>


int counter = 0;
```

```cpp
void increment_counter() {
  for (int i = 0; i < 1000000; ++i) {
    counter++; // Potential race condition here!
  }
}

int main() {
  std::thread thread1(increment_counter);
  std::thread thread2(increment_counter);

  thread1.join();
  thread2.join();

  std::cout << "Counter: " << counter << std::endl; // Expected: 2000000
  return 0;
}
```

In this example, two threads increment a shared counter variable. The counter++ operation is not atomic, meaning it involves multiple steps:

1. Read the current value of counter.
2. Increment the value.
3. Write the new value back to counter.

If both threads read the same value of counter simultaneously, then increment it, and write the result back, the final value of counter might be less than the expected 2,000,000. This is because one of the increments might be lost due to the interleaving of thread execution.

2. Data Races

A **data race** is a specific type of race condition that occurs when multiple threads access the same memory location concurrently, and at least one of the accesses is a write operation. This can lead to unpredictable and inconsistent behavior, as the value of the shared data may be corrupted or overwritten.

Data races are particularly challenging to debug because they often depend on subtle timing factors and may not manifest consistently.

3. Deadlocks

A **deadlock** occurs when two or more threads become blocked indefinitely, waiting for each other to release resources they hold. This creates a circular dependency that prevents any of the threads from progressing.

Example:

```cpp
C++

#include <iostream>
#include <thread>
#include <mutex>


std::mutex mutex1, mutex2;


void thread_function1() {
    std::lock_guard<std::mutex> lock1(mutex1); // Acquire mutex1

    // ... do some work ...

    std::lock_guard<std::mutex> lock2(mutex2); // Acquire mutex2
```

```cpp
  // ... do some more work ...

}


void thread_function2() {

  std::lock_guard<std::mutex> lock2(mutex2); // Acquire
mutex2

  // ... do some work ...

  std::lock_guard<std::mutex> lock1(mutex1); // Acquire
mutex1

  // ... do some more work ...

}


int main() {

  std::thread thread1(thread_function1);

  std::thread thread2(thread_function2);


  thread1.join();

  thread2.join();
```

```
    return 0;

}
```

In this example, thread_function1 acquires mutex1 first
and then mutex2, while thread_function2 acquires
mutex2 first and then mutex1. If both threads acquire
their first mutex simultaneously, they will then block
indefinitely waiting for the other thread to release the
second mutex, resulting in a deadlock.

Addressing the Challenges

These challenges highlight the need for careful
synchronization and coordination in concurrent
programs. Techniques such as mutexes, semaphores, and
atomic operations can be used to protect shared data and
prevent race conditions and deadlocks.

OpenMP provides high-level constructs for managing
concurrency and synchronization, making it easier to
write correct and efficient parallel programs. In the
following chapters, we will explore these constructs in
detail and learn how to apply them effectively.

Practice Problems: Basic conceptual questions about processes and threads.

Conceptual Questions:

1. **Explain the key differences between a process and a thread.**
   - ○ Focus on aspects like memory space, resource ownership, and context switching overhead.
2. **Can a process have multiple threads? Can a thread have multiple processes?**
   - ○ Explain the hierarchical relationship between processes and threads.
3. **What are the benefits of using threads instead of creating multiple processes for concurrent tasks?**
   - ○ Highlight advantages like shared memory, efficient communication, and reduced overhead.
4. **Describe a scenario where using multiple processes might be more suitable than using multiple threads.**
   - ○ Consider factors like isolation, fault tolerance, and different programming languages.
5. **Explain how concurrency can be achieved on a single-core processor.**

o Discuss the role of time-slicing and context switching in simulating parallelism.

6. **What is the relationship between concurrency and parallelism?**
   o Clarify that parallelism is a form of concurrency, but not all concurrency is parallel.

7. **Give an example of a real-world application that utilizes both concurrency and parallelism.**
   o Consider applications like web browsers, operating systems, or games.

8. **Why is it important to synchronize access to shared data in a multithreaded program?**
   o Explain the consequences of data races and race conditions.

9. **Briefly describe two common techniques for synchronizing access to shared data.**
   o Mention mutexes and semaphores as examples.

10. **What is a deadlock, and how can it occur in a multithreaded program?**
    o Provide a simple scenario illustrating a deadlock situation.

Scenario-based Questions:

1. **Imagine a web server handling multiple client requests. Would you use processes or threads to handle each request, and why?**
   - Consider factors like resource sharing, efficiency, and isolation.
2. **You are designing a video editing application. How can you use threads to improve the user experience?**
   - Think about background tasks like rendering, encoding, and applying effects.
3. **A scientific simulation needs to perform complex calculations on a large dataset. How can parallelism be used to speed up the computation?**
   - Discuss how the dataset can be divided into smaller chunks and processed concurrently.

Code-related Questions:

1. **Examine the following code snippet. Identify any potential race conditions or data races:**

```
C++
```

```
int shared_value = 0;
```

```
void thread_function() {

  for (int i = 0; i < 1000; ++i) {

    shared_value++;

  }

}
```

2. **How can you modify the code snippet above to prevent race conditions and ensure correct results?**
   - Suggest using a mutex or an atomic operation to protect the shared variable.

These practice problems encourage readers to apply their understanding of processes, threads, and the challenges of concurrent programming. By thinking critically about these concepts, they can build a solid foundation for writing efficient and correct concurrent programs with OpenMP.

Chapter 2: C++ for Concurrency

C++ Basics Refresher (Variables, Data types, Functions, Control flow - Essential for beginners)

Before we dive into the exciting world of concurrent programming with OpenMP, it's essential to have a solid grasp of the fundamentals of C++. This chapter provides a concise refresher on the core concepts, ensuring that you have the necessary foundation to build upon.

Variables: The Building Blocks

In C++, **variables** are used to store data. Think of them as containers that hold information your program needs to work with. Each variable has a specific **data type** that determines the kind of information it can store and the operations that can be performed on it.

Common Data Types:

- int: Stores whole numbers (integers), such as 10, -5, or 1000.
- float **and** double: Store decimal numbers (floating-point numbers), such as 3.14, -2.5, or 0.001.

- **char**: Stores single characters, such as 'A', '?', or '$'.
- **bool**: Stores boolean values, which can be either true or false.
- **string**: Stores sequences of characters (text), such as "Hello, world!".

Example:

```cpp
C++

int age = 30;

double price = 9.99;

char initial = 'J';

bool is_valid = true;

std::string message = "Welcome to C++!";
```

Functions: Reusable Code Blocks

Functions are blocks of code that perform a specific task. They help organize your code, make it reusable, and improve readability. Functions can take **arguments** (input values) and return a **result**.

Example:

C++

```cpp
int add(int a, int b) {

  int sum = a + b;

  return sum;

}


int main() {

  int result = add(5, 3); // Calling the add function

  std::cout << "Result: " << result << std::endl; // Output: Result: 8

  return 0;

}
```

Control Flow: Directing the Execution

Control flow statements determine the order in which your code is executed. They allow you to create conditional branches and loops, enabling your program to make decisions and repeat actions.

- if-else **statements:** Execute different blocks of code based on a condition.

C++

```cpp
if (age >= 18) {
  std::cout << "You are an adult." << std::endl;
} else {
  std::cout << "You are a minor." << std::endl;
}
```

- for **loops:** Repeat a block of code a specific number of times.

C++

```cpp
for (int i = 0; i < 5; ++i) {
  std::cout << "Iteration: " << i << std::endl;
}
```

- while **loops:** Repeat a block of code as long as a condition is true.

C++

```
int count = 0;
while (count < 10) {
  std::cout << "Count: " << count << std::endl;
  count++;
}
```

Operators: Performing Operations

C++ provides a variety of **operators** for performing operations on data.

- **Arithmetic operators:** +, -, *, /, % (modulo)
- **Comparison operators:** == (equal to), != (not equal to), >, <, >=, <=

- **Logical operators:** $\&\&$ (and), $\|$ (or), ! (not)
- **Assignment operator:** =

Example:

```cpp
C++

int x = 10;

int y = 5;

int sum = x + y; // sum is 15

bool is_equal = (x == y); // is_equal is false
```

Beyond the Basics

This refresher covers the essential C++ concepts you'll need for this book. As we delve deeper into concurrent programming, we'll encounter more advanced topics such as pointers, memory management, and object-oriented programming. These will be introduced and explained as needed, ensuring a smooth learning curve.

By mastering these fundamental building blocks, you'll be well-equipped to tackle the challenges and reap the rewards of concurrent programming with C++ and OpenMP.

Pointers and Memory Management (Crucial for understanding concurrency)

In C++, **pointers** and **memory management** are closely intertwined concepts that play a crucial role in concurrent programming. Understanding how they work is essential for writing efficient and safe multithreaded applications.

Pointers: Accessing Memory Directly

A **pointer** is a variable that stores the memory address of another variable. Think of it as a signpost that points to a specific location in the computer's memory. Pointers provide a way to directly access and manipulate data stored in memory, which can be very powerful but also requires careful handling.

Declaring and Using Pointers:

- **Declaration:** To declare a pointer, use the * symbol before the variable name. The data type of the pointer should match the data type of the variable it points to.

C++

```
int* ptr;  // Declares a pointer to an integer
```

- **Initialization:** Before using a pointer, you need to initialize it with a valid memory address. This can be done using the address-of operator (&).

C++

int num = 10;

int* ptr = # // ptr now points to the memory location of num

- **Dereferencing:** To access the value stored at the memory location pointed to by a pointer, use the dereference operator (*).

C++

int value = *ptr; // value is now 10

Memory Management: Dynamic Allocation

In C++, you can allocate memory dynamically during program execution using the new operator. This allows you to create objects and data structures whose size is not known at compile time.

Dynamic Memory Allocation:

- **new operator:** Allocates memory for a variable of a specified type and returns a pointer to that memory location.

C++

```
int* dynamic_int = new int; // Allocates memory for an integer
```

- **delete operator:** Releases memory allocated with new, preventing memory leaks.

C++

```
delete dynamic_int; // Releases the memory pointed to
by dynamic_int
```

Why Pointers and Memory Management Matter for Concurrency

In concurrent programming, multiple threads often need to access and modify shared data. Pointers provide a way to pass data between threads efficiently, avoiding the overhead of copying large objects. However, this also introduces the risk of data races and other concurrency issues.

Key Considerations for Concurrency:

- **Shared memory:** Threads within the same process share the same memory space, making it crucial to synchronize access to shared data when using pointers.
- **Data races:** If multiple threads access and modify the same memory location pointed to by a pointer without proper synchronization, data races can occur, leading to unpredictable behavior.

- **Memory leaks:** In long-running concurrent applications, failing to deallocate dynamically allocated memory can lead to memory leaks, eventually exhausting system resources.
- **Dangling pointers:** If a pointer points to memory that has been deallocated, it becomes a dangling pointer. Accessing a dangling pointer can lead to crashes or undefined behavior.

Best Practices:

- **Synchronization:** Use synchronization mechanisms like mutexes or atomic operations to protect shared data accessed through pointers.
- **Smart pointers:** Utilize smart pointers (std::unique_ptr, std::shared_ptr) to manage dynamically allocated memory automatically, reducing the risk of memory leaks and dangling pointers.
- **Thread safety:** When designing data structures or classes that will be used in a concurrent context, consider thread safety and ensure that their operations are safe to be called from multiple threads.

By understanding pointers and memory management in the context of concurrency, you can write more efficient, robust, and safe multithreaded applications. In the following chapters, we'll explore how OpenMP helps simplify concurrent programming and provides tools for managing shared memory and synchronization.

Object-Oriented Programming in C++
(Classes, Objects, Inheritance

Object-oriented programming (OOP) is a powerful paradigm that allows you to structure your code around "objects" – self-contained units that combine data and operations. While a deep dive into OOP is beyond the scope of this book, understanding its basic principles, particularly classes and objects, is valuable for writing well-organized and maintainable concurrent programs.

Classes: Blueprints for Objects

A **class** is a blueprint or template that defines the structure and behavior of objects. It encapsulates data (attributes) and functions (methods) that operate on that[1] data. Think of a class as a concept, and objects as instances of that concept.

Example:

```
C++

class Dog {

public:
```

```cpp
    std::string name;

    int age;


    void bark() {

      std::cout << "Woof!" << std::endl;

    }

};
```

In this example, Dog is a class that defines the attributes name (string) and age (integer), and the method bark(), which simulates a dog barking.

Objects: Instances of Classes

An **object** is an instance of a class. It's a concrete realization of the blueprint defined by the class. You can create multiple objects from the same class, each with its own unique data.

Example:

C++

```cpp
int main() {
```

```cpp
Dog my_dog;

my_dog.name = "Buddy";

my_dog.age = 3;

my_dog.bark(); // Output: Woof!


Dog another_dog;

another_dog.name = "Lucy";

another_dog.age = 1;

another_dog.bark(); // Output: Woof!


return 0;

}
```

Here, my_dog and another_dog are two objects of the Dog class. Each has its own name and age, and they can both perform the bark() action.

Inheritance: Extending Classes

Inheritance allows you to create new classes (derived classes) that inherit properties and behaviors from existing classes (base classes). This promotes code reuse and helps create hierarchical relationships between classes.

Example:

```cpp
C++

class Animal {
public:
 std::string name;

  void eat() {
   std::cout << "Eating..." << std::endl;
  }
};


class Dog : public Animal {
public:
  void bark() {
   std::cout << "Woof!" << std::endl;
```

```
    }

};
```

In this example, Dog inherits from Animal, so it automatically has a name attribute and the eat() method. Additionally, it has its own specific bark() method.

Relevance to Concurrency

While seemingly unrelated at first glance, OOP concepts can be very helpful in concurrent programming:

- **Encapsulation:** Classes can encapsulate data and methods, providing controlled access to shared resources and reducing the risk of data races.
- **Data protection:** You can use access modifiers (like private and protected) to restrict access to data members and ensure that they are only modified through well-defined methods, improving thread safety.
- **Code organization:** OOP promotes modularity, making it easier to structure complex concurrent programs and manage interactions between threads.
- **Design patterns:** Many concurrency design patterns, such as the Producer-Consumer pattern

or the Reader-Writer lock pattern, are best implemented using OOP techniques.

Looking Ahead

While this is a brief overview, understanding the basics of classes, objects, and inheritance will be beneficial as we move forward. As we explore OpenMP, you'll see how these concepts can be applied to design and implement concurrent programs effectively.

The C++ Standard Library (Containers, Algorithms - Introduction to useful components)

The C++ Standard Library is a treasure trove of pre-built components that can significantly boost your productivity and code quality. It provides a wide range of classes and functions for common tasks, including input/output, string manipulation, containers, and algorithms. In this section, we'll focus on containers and algorithms, which are particularly relevant for concurrent programming.

Containers: Managing Collections of Data

Containers are data structures that store and organize collections of objects. The C++ Standard Library offers a variety of containers, each with its own strengths and characteristics, allowing you to choose the most suitable one for your needs.

Commonly Used Containers:

- std::vector: A dynamic array that can grow or shrink in size as needed. Provides efficient random access to elements.
- std::list: A doubly linked list that allows efficient insertion and deletion of elements at any position.
- std::deque: A double-ended queue that supports efficient insertion and deletion at both ends.
- std::set: Stores a sorted set of unique elements.
- std::map: Stores key-value pairs, where each key is associated with a value. Allows efficient lookup of values based on their keys.

Example:

C++

```
#include <vector>

#include <iostream>


int main() {
  std::vector<int> numbers = {1, 5, 2, 8, 3};
```

```cpp
    // Accessing elements

    std::cout << "First element: " << numbers[0] << std::endl; // Output: 1


    // Adding elements

    numbers.push_back(10);


    // Iterating over elements

    for (int number : numbers) {

      std::cout << number << " ";

    }

    std::cout << std::endl; // Output: 1 5 2 8 3 10


    return 0;

}
```

Algorithms: Performing Operations on Data

Algorithms are functions that perform operations on data, often in conjunction with containers. The C++ Standard Library provides a rich set of algorithms for tasks such as searching, sorting, transforming, and manipulating data.

Commonly Used Algorithms:

- std::sort: Sorts a range of elements in ascending order.
- std::find: Searches for a specific value in a range of elements.
- std::for_each: Applies a function to each element in a range.
- std::transform: Applies a transformation function to each element in a range.
- std::accumulate: Calculates the sum (or other accumulation) of elements in a range.

Example:

```C++
#include <vector>

#include <algorithm>

#include <iostream>
```

```cpp
int main() {

  std::vector<int> numbers = {5, 2, 8, 1, 3};


  // Sorting the vector

  std::sort(numbers.begin(), numbers.end());


  // Printing the sorted vector

  for (int number : numbers) {

    std::cout << number << " ";

  }

  std::cout << std::endl; // Output: 1 2 3 5 8


  return 0;

}
```

Relevance to Concurrency

The C++ Standard Library containers and algorithms are valuable tools for concurrent programming:

- **Thread safety:** Some containers and algorithms have thread safety guarantees, making them suitable for use in multithreaded environments.
- **Efficiency:** Standard Library components are highly optimized, contributing to the performance of your concurrent code.
- **Data structures:** Containers provide efficient ways to store and manage shared data accessed by multiple threads.
- **Parallel algorithms:** C++17 introduced parallel algorithms that can leverage multiple cores to perform operations concurrently, further enhancing performance.

By utilizing the C++ Standard Library effectively, you can write cleaner, more efficient, and more maintainable concurrent code. As we delve into OpenMP, you'll see how these components can be combined with OpenMP constructs to create powerful parallel applications.

Code Samples: Examples of C++ code demonstrating core concepts.

C++

```cpp
#include <iostream>

#include <vector>

#include <algorithm>
```

```cpp
// Function to calculate the factorial of a
number

int factorial(int n) {

  if (n == 0) {

    return 1;

  } else {

    return n * factorial(n - 1);

  }

}


int main() {

  // Variables and data types

  int age = 25;

  double price = 19.99;

  char initial = 'A';

  bool is_valid = true;

  std::string name = "John Doe";


  std::cout << "Age: " << age << std::endl;
```

```cpp
    std::cout << "Price: " << price <<
std::endl;

    std::cout << "Initial: " << initial <<
std::endl;

    std::cout << "Is valid: " << is_valid <<
std::endl;

    std::cout << "Name: " << name <<
std::endl;


    // Control flow (if-else)

    if (age >= 18) {

        std::cout << "You are an adult." <<
std::endl;

    } else {

        std::cout << "You are a minor." <<
std::endl;

    }


    // Control flow (for loop)

    for (int i = 0; i < 5; ++i) {

        std::cout << "Iteration: " << i <<
std::endl;

    }
```

```cpp
    // Function call

    int result = factorial(5);

    std::cout << "Factorial of 5: " << result
<< std::endl;


    // Vectors (dynamic arrays)

    std::vector<int> numbers = {10, 5, 20,
15};

    std::cout << "Numbers: ";

    for (int number : numbers) {

      std::cout << number << " ";

    }

    std::cout << std::endl;


    // Sorting a vector

                   std::sort(numbers.begin(),
numbers.end());

    std::cout << "Sorted numbers: ";

    for (int number : numbers) {

      std::cout << number << " ";
```

```
    }

    std::cout << std::endl;


    return 0;

}
```

This code demonstrates:

- **Variables and data types:** int, double, char, bool, std::string
- **Control flow:** if-else, for loop
- **Functions:** factorial function with recursion
- **Vectors:** Creating, accessing, and modifying a std::vector
- **Algorithms:** Using std::sort to sort a vector

This is just a small sample of the many things you can do with C++. As we progress through the book, you'll encounter more complex and interesting examples that demonstrate the full power of the language, especially in the context of concurrent programming.

Practice Problems: C++ coding exercises to reinforce basic understanding.

Here are some practice problems designed to reinforce the C++ basics covered in this chapter:

1. Temperature Conversion:

- Write a program that prompts the user to enter a temperature in Celsius and converts it to Fahrenheit.[1] The conversion formula is:[2] F = (C * 9/5) + 32.

2. Even or Odd:

- Write a program that prompts the user to enter an integer and determines whether it's even or odd. Use the modulo operator (%) to check for divisibility by 2.

3. Calculate Area:

- Write a program that calculates the area of a rectangle. Prompt the user to enter the length and width of the rectangle.

4. Grade Calculator:

- Write a program that prompts the user to enter a numerical grade (0-100) and assigns a letter grade based on the following scale:

- 90-100: A
- 80-89: B
- 70-79: C
- 60-69: D
- Below 60: F

5. Factorial Calculation:

- Write a program that calculates the factorial of a non-negative integer entered by the user. The factorial of n (denoted by n!) is the product of all positive integers less than or equal to n. For example, $5! = 5 * 4 * 3 * 2 * 1 = 120.$[3]

6. Reverse a String:

- Write a program that prompts the user to enter a string and then prints the reverse of that string.

7. Sum of Array Elements:

- Write a program that calculates the sum of all elements in an array of integers.

8. Find the Largest Element:

- Write a program that finds the largest element in an array of integers.

9. Simple Calculator:

- Write a program that simulates a simple calculator. It should prompt the user to enter two numbers and an operator (+, -, *, /) and then perform the corresponding operation.

10. Fibonacci Sequence:

- Write a program that prints the first n numbers in the Fibonacci sequence, where n is a value entered by the user. In the Fibonacci sequence, each number is the sum of the two preceding ones (e.g., 0, 1, 1, 2, 3, 5, 8...).

These problems encourage readers to apply the C++ concepts covered in this chapter, including variables, data types, operators, control flow, and functions. By working through these exercises, they will gain valuable hands-on experience and solidify their understanding of the language fundamentals.

Part II: Introducing OpenMP

Chapter 3: Getting Started with OpenMP

What is OpenMP? (History, Benefits)

OpenMP (Open Multi-Processing) is a powerful API (Application Programming Interface) that provides a simple and flexible way to write parallel programs for shared-memory multicore architectures.[1] It consists of a set of compiler directives, library routines, and environment variables that extend C, C++, and Fortran to express parallelism.[2]

In essence, OpenMP allows you to parallelize your code by adding special directives (comments that start with #pragma omp) to your source code. These directives instruct the compiler to generate multithreaded code that can take advantage of multiple cores, enabling your programs to run faster and more efficiently.

A Brief History

The roots of OpenMP can be traced back to the late 1990s when a group of hardware and software vendors, including industry giants like Intel, IBM, and SGI, recognized the need for a standardized approach to shared-memory parallel programming.[3]

- **1997:** The OpenMP Architecture Review Board (ARB) released the first OpenMP specification for Fortran 1.0.[4]
- **1998:** OpenMP for C/C++ 1.0 was released.
- **2000 - 2008:** OpenMP 2.0 and 2.5 were released, introducing new features and expanding support for both C/C++ and Fortran.[5]
- **2011 - Present:** OpenMP 3.0, 3.1, 4.0, 4.5, 5.0, 5.1, and 5.2 have been released, bringing significant enhancements such as tasks, accelerator support, and improved error handling.

OpenMP has become a widely adopted standard, supported by major compilers like GCC, Intel, and Clang.[6] Its ongoing development and evolution ensure its relevance in the ever-changing landscape of parallel computing.

Benefits of OpenMP

OpenMP offers numerous advantages that make it a compelling choice for parallel programming:

- **Simplicity:** OpenMP's directive-based approach is relatively easy to learn and use, especially compared to lower-level threading models. You can incrementally parallelize your code by adding directives to existing serial code, often without major restructuring.[7]

- **Portability:** OpenMP is a portable standard, meaning your code can be compiled and run on different platforms and operating systems with minimal changes.[8]
- **Flexibility:** OpenMP supports both fine-grained and coarse-grained parallelism, allowing you to parallelize loops, regions of code, or even individual tasks.[9]
- **Performance:** By utilizing multiple cores, OpenMP can significantly improve the performance of your applications, especially for computationally intensive tasks.[10]
- **Incremental Parallelization:** You can start with a serial program and gradually add OpenMP directives to parallelize critical sections, making it easier to manage and test the parallelization process.
- **Directives for Data Handling:** OpenMP provides directives for managing data sharing and synchronization, helping you avoid common concurrency pitfalls like race conditions and deadlocks.[11]

OpenMP empowers developers to harness the power of multicore processors without the complexities of low-level thread management. Its ease of use, portability, and performance benefits make it an excellent choice for a wide range of applications, from scientific simulations and image processing to financial modeling and data analysis.

Setting up Your OpenMP Environment (Compiler support, Compilation flags)

Before you can start writing and compiling OpenMP programs, you need to ensure that your development environment is properly set up. This involves having a compiler that supports OpenMP and knowing the necessary compilation flags to enable OpenMP features.

Compiler Support

Most modern C++ compilers support OpenMP, including:

- **GCC (GNU Compiler Collection):** A widely used open-source compiler available on Linux, macOS, and Windows.
- **Clang:** Another popular open-source compiler known for its fast compile times and helpful error messages.
- **Intel C++ Compiler:** A commercial compiler optimized for Intel processors, often offering excellent performance for computationally intensive applications.

- **Microsoft Visual C++:** The compiler included with Microsoft Visual Studio, supporting OpenMP on Windows.

It's important to use a recent version of your chosen compiler to ensure that you have access to the latest OpenMP features and optimizations.

Compilation Flags

To enable OpenMP support during compilation, you need to use specific compilation flags. These flags tell the compiler to process OpenMP directives and generate parallel code.

- **GCC and Clang:** Use the -fopenmp flag.

Bash

```
g++ -fopenmp my_program.cpp -o my_program

clang++ -fopenmp my_program.cpp -o my_program
```

- **Intel C++ Compiler:** Use the -qopenmp flag.

Bash

```
icpc -qopenmp my_program.cpp -o my_program
```

- **Microsoft Visual C++:** Enable OpenMP support in the project properties.
  1. Go to Project Properties -> C/C++ -> Language.
  2. Set "Open MP Support" to "Yes".

Verification

To verify that your environment is set up correctly, you can compile and run a simple OpenMP program like the "Hello, World!" example we'll see in the next section. If the program compiles and runs without errors, and you see output from multiple threads, then your OpenMP environment is ready to go!

Integrated Development Environments (IDEs)

If you're using an IDE, you might need to configure the IDE to use the appropriate compiler and compilation flags. Most IDEs provide settings for customizing the build process.

Troubleshooting

If you encounter issues during compilation, double-check that:

- You have a compatible compiler with OpenMP support.
- You are using the correct compilation flags for your compiler.
- Your IDE is configured correctly to use the OpenMP-enabled compiler.

With your OpenMP environment set up, you're ready to start writing parallel programs that can harness the full power of your multicore system.

Your First OpenMP Program ("Hello, World!" example with detailed explanations)

Let's dive into the world of OpenMP with a classic "Hello, World!" example. This simple program demonstrates the fundamental concept of creating parallel regions and executing code on multiple threads.

C++

```cpp
#include <iostream>

#include <omp.h> // Include the OpenMP header file
```

```cpp
int main() {

  #pragma omp parallel

  {

      std::cout << "Hello, World! from thread " <<
  omp_get_thread_num() << std::endl;

  }

  return 0;

}
```

Explanation:

1. #include <omp.h>: This line includes the OpenMP header file, which provides the necessary declarations for using OpenMP functions and directives.

2. #pragma omp parallel: This is the key OpenMP directive that creates a parallel region. When the program encounters this directive, it creates a team of threads, and the code within the curly braces {} is executed by each thread in parallel.

3. omp_get_thread_num(): This OpenMP function returns the thread ID of the current thread. Thread IDs typically start from 0 and increment for each thread in the team.

4. std::cout << ... << std::endl;: This line prints the "Hello, World!" message along with the thread ID to the console. Since each thread executes this line, you'll see multiple greetings, each with a different thread ID.

Compiling and Running

Remember to compile this code with the appropriate OpenMP flag for your compiler (e.g., -fopenmp for GCC/Clang). When you run the program, you should see output similar to this:

Hello, World! from thread 2

Hello, World! from thread 0

Hello, World! from thread 1

Hello, World! from thread 3

The order of the output might vary because the operating system schedules threads in a non-deterministic way. The number of threads created depends on several factors, including the number of cores in your system and any environment variables that might influence OpenMP's behavior.

Breaking it Down

This simple example illustrates the core idea of OpenMP:

- **Parallel regions:** You define sections of code that should be executed in parallel using the #pragma omp parallel directive.
- **Thread teams:** OpenMP creates a team of threads to execute the parallel region.
- **Thread identification:** You can use omp_get_thread_num() to identify each thread within the team.

By understanding this basic structure, you can start to apply OpenMP to parallelize more complex and interesting code. In the next sections, we'll explore how to control the number of threads, distribute work among threads, and manage shared data.

The #pragma omp parallel Directive (Creating threads, Work-sharing)

The #pragma omp parallel directive is the cornerstone of OpenMP. It's the gateway to creating parallel regions within your code, enabling you to harness the power of multiple threads and execute tasks concurrently. Let's delve deeper into its mechanics and explore how it works.

Creating Threads

When the compiler encounters a #pragma omp parallel directive, it generates code to create a team of threads. The code enclosed within the directive's associated structured block (typically defined by curly braces {}) becomes the **parallel region**. Each thread in the team executes the code within this parallel region.

C++

```cpp
#pragma omp parallel
{
    // Code to be executed by each thread in parallel
}
```

Number of Threads

By default, OpenMP creates a number of threads equal to the number of logical cores available on your system. However, you can control the number of threads using various methods:

- **Environment variables:** The OMP_NUM_THREADS environment variable allows you to specify the desired number of threads.

Bash

```bash
export OMP_NUM_THREADS=4  // Sets the number of threads to 4
```

- omp_set_num_threads() **function:** This function, available in the omp.h header, allows you to set the number of threads programmatically.

C++

```cpp
omp_set_num_threads(8); // Sets the number of threads to 8
```

- num_threads **clause:** You can use the num_threads clause within the #pragma omp parallel directive itself to specify the number of threads for that particular parallel region.

C++

```
#pragma omp parallel num_threads(6)

{

    // Code to be executed by 6 threads

}
```

Work-Sharing: Distributing Tasks

While the #pragma omp parallel directive creates multiple threads, it doesn't automatically divide the work among them. By default, each thread executes the entire parallel region. To distribute work effectively, you need to use **work-sharing constructs**.

OpenMP provides several work-sharing constructs, including:

- #pragma omp for: Distributes iterations of a for loop among the threads in the team.
- #pragma omp sections: Divides a block of code into sections, with each thread executing a different section.
- #pragma omp tasks: Creates tasks that can be dynamically assigned to threads.

We'll explore these work-sharing constructs in detail in the upcoming chapters.

Implicit Barrier

An important aspect of the #pragma omp parallel directive is the **implicit barrier** at the end of the parallel region. This barrier ensures that all threads in the team have finished executing the parallel region before any thread proceeds to the code after the parallel region.

Example with Work-Sharing:

C++

```cpp
#include <iostream>
#include <omp.h>

int main() {
  #pragma omp parallel
  {
    #pragma omp for
    for (int i = 0; i < 10; ++i) {
      std::cout << "Thread " << omp_get_thread_num() <<
" processing iteration " << i << std::endl;
```

```
    }

  }

  return 0;

}
```

In this example, the #pragma omp for directive distributes the iterations of the for loop among the threads, ensuring that each iteration is executed by only one thread.

Key Takeaways

The #pragma omp parallel directive is the foundation for parallel programming with OpenMP. It allows you to create threads, define parallel regions, and, in conjunction with work-sharing constructs, distribute tasks among threads effectively. Understanding its behavior and options is crucial for writing efficient and scalable parallel programs.

Code Samples: Simple OpenMP programs with variations.

C++

```cpp
// Example 1: Basic "Hello, World!" with 4
threads

#include <iostream>

#include <omp.h>


int main() {

  omp_set_num_threads(4); // Set the number
of threads to 4


  #pragma omp parallel

  {

    int thread_id = omp_get_thread_num();

      std::cout << "Hello from thread " <<
thread_id << std::endl;

  }


  return 0;

}
```

C++

```cpp
// Example 2: Calculating the sum of an
array in parallel


#include <iostream>

#include <vector>

#include <omp.h>


int main() {
    std::vector<int> numbers = {1, 2, 3, 4,
5, 6, 7, 8, 9, 10};

    int sum = 0;


    #pragma omp parallel for reduction(+:sum)

    for (int i = 0; i < numbers.size(); ++i)
{

        sum += numbers[i];

    }


    std::cout << "Sum: " << sum << std::endl;
// Output: Sum: 55

    return 0;
```

```
}
```

C++

```cpp
// Example 3: Parallel sections for
different tasks


#include <iostream>

#include <omp.h>


int main() {

  #pragma omp parallel

  {

    #pragma omp sections

    {

      #pragma omp section

      {

              std::cout << "Thread " <<
omp_get_thread_num() << " executing Section
1" << std::endl;

        // ... perform task 1 ...

      }
```

```
#pragma omp section

    {

            std::cout << "Thread " <<
omp_get_thread_num() << " executing Section
2" << std::endl;

        // ... perform task 2 ...

    }

  }

}

  return 0;

}
```

These examples demonstrate different ways to use
OpenMP directives:

- **Example 1:** Shows how to set the number of
  threads and print a message from each thread.
- **Example 2:** Demonstrates how to parallelize a
  loop to calculate the sum of an array using the
  reduction clause.
- **Example 3:** Illustrates how to use sections to
  divide work into different tasks executed by
  different threads.

By experimenting with these examples and modifying them, you can gain a better understanding of how OpenMP works and how to apply it to your own code.

Practice Problems: Modifying and extending the "Hello, World!" example.

These practice problems will help you solidify your understanding of the #pragma omp parallel directive and explore its capabilities:

1. Controlled Thread Count:

- Modify the "Hello, World!" example to use the omp_set_num_threads() function to create 8 threads.
- Run the program and observe the output. How many "Hello, World!" messages do you see?
- Experiment with different values for omp_set_num_threads().

2. Environment Variable Control:

- Set the OMP_NUM_THREADS environment variable to 6 before running the "Hello, World!" program.
- Observe the output. How many threads are created now?
- Try changing the environment variable to different values.

3. num_threads **Clause:**

- Modify the "Hello, World!" example to use the num_threads clause within the #pragma omp parallel directive to create 5 threads.
- Compile and run the program. Verify that the output shows 5 threads.

4. Printing Thread IDs and Processor IDs:

- Extend the "Hello, World!" example to print both the thread ID (omp_get_thread_num()) and the processor ID (sched_getcpu()) for each thread. (You'll need to include the <sched.h> header for sched_getcpu()).
- Observe the output. Do threads always run on the same processor?

5. Simple Parallel Loop:

- Create a program with a for loop that iterates 10 times. Inside the loop, print the loop iteration counter (i) and the thread ID.
- Add a #pragma omp parallel directive before the loop. Run the program and observe the output. Does each thread execute all iterations of the loop?
- Now, add a #pragma omp for directive immediately before the for loop. Run the program again. What difference do you observe

in the output? (This introduces the concept of work-sharing, which we'll explore further in the next chapter.)

6. Timing Experiment:

- Write a program that performs a time-consuming calculation (e.g., calculating the factorial of a large number) inside a for loop.
- Measure the execution time of the program without OpenMP.
- Add OpenMP directives to parallelize the loop.
- Measure the execution time again. Do you see a performance improvement? Experiment with different numbers of threads.

Challenge Problem:

- Create a program that generates a random number between 1 and 100 within each thread of a parallel region.
- Ensure that each thread generates a different random number (hint: you might need to use a thread-safe random number generator or synchronize access to the random number generation).

These practice problems encourage you to actively experiment with the #pragma omp parallel directive, manipulate the number of threads, and observe the effects of parallelism. This hands-on experience will build your confidence and prepare you for more advanced OpenMP concepts.

Chapter 4: Parallel Loops and Work-Sharing

The #pragma omp for Directive (Distributing loop iterations)

One of the most common patterns in parallel programming is dividing the iterations of a loop among multiple threads. This is where the #pragma omp for directive shines in OpenMP. It provides a simple and effective way to parallelize loops, enabling you to distribute the workload and potentially achieve significant speedups.

Basic Usage

The #pragma omp for directive is a work-sharing construct that must be enclosed within a #pragma omp parallel region. It instructs the compiler to distribute the iterations of the immediately following for loop among the threads in the team.

C++

```
#pragma omp parallel

{

   #pragma omp for
```

```
for (int i = 0; i < n; ++i) {

    // Code to be executed for each iteration

    }

}
```

In this example, the for loop with n iterations will be executed in parallel by the threads in the team. Each thread will be responsible for a subset of the iterations.

Iteration Distribution

OpenMP provides flexibility in how loop iterations are distributed among threads. The default behavior is typically **static scheduling**, where iterations are divided into chunks of roughly equal size, and each chunk is assigned to a thread. However, you can control the scheduling using different clauses:

- schedule(static, chunk_size): Divides the iterations into chunks of size chunk_size and assigns them to threads in a round-robin fashion.
- schedule(dynamic, chunk_size): Dynamically assigns chunks of size chunk_size to threads as they become available. This can be helpful when iterations have varying workloads.

- schedule(guided, chunk_size): Similar to dynamic scheduling, but the chunk size decreases exponentially as the computation progresses. This can provide a good balance between load balancing and overhead.
- schedule(auto): Lets the compiler or runtime environment decide the best scheduling strategy.

Example with Dynamic Scheduling:

C++

```cpp
#pragma omp parallel
{
  #pragma omp for schedule(dynamic, 5)
  for (int i = 0; i < 100; ++i) {
    // Code with potentially varying workload per iteration
  }
}
```

In this example, chunks of 5 iterations are dynamically assigned to threads as they become available.

Important Considerations

- **Loop Variables:** The loop variable (i in the examples) is implicitly made private to each thread. This means each thread has its own copy of the loop variable.
- **Data Dependencies:** Be mindful of data dependencies between iterations. If iterations depend on results from previous iterations, you might need to use synchronization mechanisms to ensure correct execution.
- **Reductions:** If you need to combine results from different iterations (e.g., calculate a sum or find a maximum), use the reduction clause, which we'll discuss in the next section.

Benefits of #pragma omp for

- **Simplicity:** Parallelizing loops is straightforward with the #pragma omp for directive.
- **Efficiency:** OpenMP handles the work distribution and thread management, allowing you to focus on the core logic of your code.
- **Flexibility:** You can control the scheduling strategy to optimize for different workload distributions.

By mastering the #pragma omp for directive, you can effectively parallelize loops and unlock the performance potential of your multicore system. In the following sections, we'll explore related concepts like loop scheduling, reductions, and data handling in more detail.

Loop Scheduling (Static, Dynamic, Guided - Explained with code)

When parallelizing loops with #pragma omp for, you have the power to control how iterations are divided among threads. This is called **loop scheduling**, and it plays a crucial role in achieving optimal performance. OpenMP offers several scheduling strategies, each with its own characteristics and trade-offs.

1. Static Scheduling

Static scheduling is the default in most OpenMP implementations. It divides the iterations into chunks of roughly equal size and assigns them to threads in a round-robin fashion. This approach is simple and has low overhead, but it may not be optimal if the workload varies significantly between iterations.

Code Example:

C++

```
#pragma omp parallel
{
```

```
#pragma omp for schedule(static, 5) // Chunk size of 5

for (int i = 0; i < 100; ++i) {

// Code to be executed for each iteration

}

}
```

In this example, the 100 iterations are divided into chunks of 5. If you have 4 threads, thread 0 gets iterations 0-4, 20-24, 40-44, 60-64, and 80-84. Thread 1 gets 5-9, 25-29, and so on.

2. Dynamic Scheduling

Dynamic scheduling assigns chunks of iterations to threads dynamically as they become available. This is useful when the workload per iteration varies significantly, as it allows threads to pick up new chunks as they finish their current ones, leading to better load balancing.

Code Example:

C++

```
#pragma omp parallel
```

```cpp
{
    #pragma omp for schedule(dynamic, 10) // Chunk size
    of 10

    for (int i = 0; i < 100; ++i) {

    // Code with potentially varying workload per iteration

    }

}
```

Here, chunks of 10 iterations are assigned to threads as they become idle. If one thread finishes its chunk quickly, it can immediately request another chunk, ensuring that all threads are kept busy.

3. Guided Scheduling

Guided scheduling is a variant of dynamic scheduling where the chunk size decreases exponentially as the computation progresses. This approach starts with large chunks to reduce overhead and gradually reduces the chunk size to improve load balancing towards the end of the loop.

Code Example:

C++

```
#pragma omp parallel

{

  #pragma omp for schedule(guided, 8) // Initial chunk
size of 8

  for (int i = 0; i < 100; ++i) {

    // Code to be executed for each iteration

  }

}
```

This starts with chunks of size 8 (or larger, adjusted based on the number of iterations and threads). As threads complete chunks, they receive smaller chunks, ensuring that work is distributed more evenly as the loop progresses.

Choosing the Right Schedule

The best scheduling strategy depends on the characteristics of your loop and the workload distribution:

- **Static:** Suitable for loops with relatively even workload per iteration.

- **Dynamic:** Best for loops with unpredictable or highly variable workload per iteration.
- **Guided:** A good compromise between static and dynamic, often providing good performance for a variety of workloads.

You can experiment with different scheduling strategies and chunk sizes to find the optimal configuration for your specific application. Profiling tools can help you analyze the performance and identify any load imbalances.

Reductions (Efficiently combining results from parallel loops)

When you parallelize a loop with #pragma omp for, each thread typically works on a subset of the iterations independently. But what if you need to combine the results from all iterations, such as calculating a sum, finding a maximum value, or performing a logical AND operation? This is where **reductions** come in.

The reduction **Clause**

The reduction clause in OpenMP provides a concise and efficient way to perform reductions on variables within parallel loops. It specifies an operator and a variable that will be used to accumulate the results from all threads.

Syntax:

C++

#**pragma** omp for reduction(operator:variable)

- operator**:** The reduction operator (e.g., +, *, -, max, min, &&, ||).
- variable**:** The variable that will hold the final reduced value.

Example: Summing an Array

C++

```
#include <iostream>

#include <vector>

#include <omp.h>


int main() {
  std::vector<int> numbers = {1, 2, 3, 4, 5, 6, 7, 8, 9, 10};
  int sum = 0;
```

```
#pragma omp parallel for reduction(+:sum)

for (int i = 0; i < numbers.size(); ++i) {

  sum += numbers[i];

}


  std::cout << "Sum: " << sum << std::endl; // Output:
Sum: 55

  return 0;

}
```

In this example, the reduction(+:sum) clause tells
OpenMP to perform a sum reduction on the sum
variable. Each thread will have its own private copy of
sum, and at the end of the loop, these private copies will
be combined using[1] the + operator to produce the final
result in the original sum variable.

How Reductions Work

OpenMP handles reductions efficiently by:

1. **Creating private copies:** Each thread gets a
   private copy of the reduction variable.

2. **Accumulating locally:** Each thread performs the reduction operation on its private copy.
3. **Combining results:** At the end of the parallel region, OpenMP combines the private copies using the specified operator to produce the final result.

Benefits of Reductions

- **Conciseness:** The reduction clause provides a clear and concise way to express reductions.
- **Efficiency:** OpenMP optimizes the reduction operation, often using specialized instructions or algorithms for faster execution.
- **Correctness:** Reductions ensure that the final result is correct, regardless of the order in which threads execute the loop iterations.

Supported Operators

OpenMP supports a variety of reduction operators, including:

- **Arithmetic:** +, *, -
- **Logical:** &&, ||
- **Bitwise:** &, |, ^
- **Comparison:** max, min

Beyond Simple Reductions

OpenMP also allows you to define your own reduction operations using user-defined functions. This provides flexibility for more complex scenarios.

By understanding and utilizing reductions, you can efficiently combine results from parallel loops and write concise and performant OpenMP code.

Common Mistakes: Race conditions in loops, Incorrect reductions.

While OpenMP simplifies parallel programming, it's still crucial to be aware of common pitfalls that can lead to incorrect results or performance issues. Here are some frequent mistakes to avoid when working with parallel loops and reductions:

1. Race Conditions in Loops

Race conditions occur when multiple threads access and modify shared data simultaneously, leading to unpredictable and erroneous[1] results. This is especially common in loops where iterations depend on shared variables.

Example:

C++

```cpp
int total = 0;

#pragma omp parallel for
for (int i = 0; i < 100; ++i) {
  total += i; // Race condition!
}
```

In this example, the total variable is shared, and multiple threads try to update it concurrently. This can result in lost updates, as the += operation is not atomic.

Solution:

Use a reduction clause to handle the accumulation safely:

C++

```cpp
#pragma omp parallel for reduction(+:total)
for (int i = 0; i < 100; ++i) {
  total += i; // Now safe with reduction
}
```

Alternatively, you can use critical sections or atomic operations to protect the shared variable.

2. Incorrect Reductions

Using the wrong reduction operator or applying a reduction to a variable that shouldn't be reduced can lead to incorrect results.

Example:

C++

```
int max_value = 0;


#pragma omp parallel for reduction(+:max_value) // Incorrect operator!
for (int i = 0; i < 100; ++i) {
  if (array[i] > max_value) {
    max_value = array[i];
  }
}
```

In this case, the + operator is not suitable for finding the maximum value.

Solution:

Use the max operator instead:

C++

```
#pragma omp parallel for reduction(max:max_value) // Correct operator
for (int i = 0; i < 100; ++i) {
  if (array[i] > max_value) {
    max_value = array[i];
  }
}
```

3. Forgetting Private Variables

If variables within a parallel loop need to be unique to each thread, you must declare them as private. Otherwise, threads might interfere with each other's data.

Example:

C++

```cpp
int temp = 0;

#pragma omp parallel for
for (int i = 0; i < 100; ++i) {
    temp = calculate_value(i); // Potential issue if temp is shared
    // ... use temp ...
}
```

Solution:

Declare temp as private using the private clause:

C++

```cpp
#pragma omp parallel for private(temp)
for (int i = 0; i < 100; ++i) {
    int temp = calculate_value(i); // Now temp is private to each thread
    // ... use temp ...
```

}

4. Ignoring Loop Dependencies

If iterations of a loop depend on results from previous iterations, parallelizing the loop directly can lead to incorrect results.

Example:

C++

```cpp
#pragma omp parallel for
for (int i = 1; i < 100; ++i) {
    array[i] = array[i - 1] + i; // Dependency on previous iteration
}
```

Solution:

In such cases, you might need to restructure the code, use different parallelization techniques (like tasks), or apply synchronization mechanisms to ensure correct execution.

5. Over-Parallelization

Parallelizing everything might not always lead to better performance. The overhead of creating threads and managing parallelism can sometimes outweigh the benefits, especially for small loops or simple computations.

Solution:

Profile your code to identify performance bottlenecks and focus on parallelizing the most computationally intensive parts.

By being mindful of these common mistakes, you can write more correct, efficient, and reliable parallel programs with OpenMP. Careful consideration of data sharing, synchronization, and loop dependencies is crucial for successful parallel execution.

Code Samples: Examples demonstrating different loop scheduling techniques and reductions.

C++

```
// Example 1: Static Scheduling
```

```cpp
#include <iostream>

#include <vector>

#include <omp.h>


int main() {

    std::vector<int> data(100, 1); // Initialize a vector with 100 elements, each with value 1


    #pragma omp parallel for schedule(static, 10)
    for (int i = 0; i < data.size(); ++i) {
      data[i] = i * 2;
        std::cout << "Thread " << omp_get_thread_num() << " processed element " << i << std::endl;

    }


    return 0;
}
```

In this example, schedule(static, 10) divides the 100 iterations into chunks of 10. Each thread receives consecutive chunks of iterations. You'll likely see each thread processing a contiguous block of elements.

C++

```cpp
// Example 2: Dynamic Scheduling

#include <iostream>
#include <vector>
#include <omp.h>

int main() {
  std::vector<int> data(100, 1);


  #pragma omp parallel for schedule(dynamic, 5)
  for (int i = 0; i < data.size(); ++i) {
    // Simulate varying workload (some iterations take longer)
    if (i % 2 == 0) {
```

```cpp
    // Simulate a longer operation for even iterations

    for (int j = 0; j < 1000000; ++j) {}

    }

  data[i] = i * 2;

    std::cout << "Thread " << omp_get_thread_num() <<
" processed element " << i << std::endl;

  }


  return 0;

}
```

Here, schedule(dynamic, 5) assigns chunks of 5 iterations to threads as they become available. Due to the simulated varying workload, you'll observe that threads might process elements in a less predictable order, as threads that finish faster pick up new chunks.

C++

```cpp
// Example 3: Guided Scheduling
```

```cpp
#include <iostream>
#include <vector>
#include <omp.h>

int main() {
  std::vector<int> data(100, 1);

  #pragma omp parallel for schedule(guided, 10)
  for (int i = 0; i < data.size(); ++i) {
    data[i] = i * 2;
    std::cout << "Thread " << omp_get_thread_num() <<
" processed element " << i << std::endl;

  }


  return 0;

}
```

With schedule(guided, 10), the initial chunk size is 10, but it decreases exponentially as threads complete their work. You might see threads starting with larger chunks and then receiving smaller chunks towards the end.

C++

```cpp
// Example 4: Reduction (sum)


#include <iostream>
#include <vector>
#include <omp.h>


int main() {
  std::vector<int> data = {1, 2, 3, 4, 5, 6, 7, 8, 9, 10};
  int sum = 0;


  #pragma omp parallel for reduction(+:sum)
  for (int i = 0; i < data.size(); ++i) {
    sum += data[i];
  }
```

```
    std::cout << "Sum of elements: " << sum << std::endl;
// Output: 55

    return 0;

}
```

This example demonstrates a sum reduction using reduction(+:sum). Each thread has a private copy of sum, accumulates its portion of the sum, and finally, the private copies are added together to produce the total sum.

These examples provide concrete illustrations of how different loop scheduling techniques and reductions work in OpenMP. By experimenting with these code snippets and observing the output, you can gain a deeper understanding of how to apply these concepts effectively in your parallel programs.

Practice Problems: Parallelizing loops with varying workloads.

These practice problems will challenge you to apply different loop scheduling techniques to optimize the parallelization of loops with uneven workloads:

1. Simulate Varying Workloads:

- Create a for loop that iterates 100 times.
- Inside the loop, introduce a conditional statement (e.g., if (i % 2 == 0)) to simulate a longer computation for some iterations (e.g., even iterations). You can use a nested loop or a sleep function to artificially increase the execution time of these iterations.
- Parallelize the loop using #pragma omp parallel for with schedule(static).
- Measure the execution time.
- Now, change the scheduling to dynamic and guided. Experiment with different chunk sizes.
- Compare the execution times for different scheduling strategies. Which one performs best, and why?

2. Process an Image:

- Load an image (e.g., using a library like OpenCV).
- Create a for loop to iterate over the pixels of the image.
- Inside the loop, perform an operation on each pixel that has varying computational complexity. For example, you could apply a filter that is more computationally intensive for certain colors or regions of the image.
- Parallelize the loop using different scheduling strategies and chunk sizes.

- Measure the execution time for each strategy. Analyze the results and determine which scheduling approach is most effective for this task.

3. Monte Carlo Simulation:

- Implement a Monte Carlo simulation (e.g., estimating the value of pi) using a for loop.
- Introduce some randomness in the workload of each iteration. For example, you could have some iterations perform more calculations or generate more random numbers than others.
- Parallelize the loop using different scheduling strategies.
- Measure the execution time and compare the results. How does the choice of scheduling affect the performance of the simulation?

4. Analyze a Text File:

- Read a large text file.
- Create a for loop to process each line of the file.
- Simulate varying workloads by performing more complex operations on certain lines (e.g., lines that contain specific keywords or patterns).
- Parallelize the loop using different scheduling strategies.

- Measure the execution time and analyze the performance. Which scheduling strategy is most suitable for this scenario, and why?

5. Sorting with Varying Comparisons:

- Implement a sorting algorithm (e.g., bubble sort or insertion sort) using a for loop.
- Introduce varying workloads by making the comparison operation more complex for certain elements (e.g., comparing strings instead of numbers, or performing more detailed comparisons).
- Parallelize the loop using different scheduling strategies.
- Measure the execution time and analyze the results. How does the choice of scheduling affect the performance of the sorting algorithm?

By working through these problems, you'll gain valuable experience in applying different loop scheduling techniques to optimize parallel loops with varying workloads. Remember to analyze the results and understand the trade-offs between different scheduling strategies in the context of your specific application.

Chapter 5: Data Handling and Synchronization

Shared vs. Private Variables (Understanding data scope in OpenMP)

When writing parallel programs with OpenMP, it's crucial to understand how data is shared or kept private among threads. This concept of **data scope** determines which variables are accessible to all threads and which are isolated within each thread.[1] Proper management of data scope is essential for preventing race conditions, ensuring correctness, and optimizing performance.

Shared Variables: Accessible to All

By default, most variables declared outside of parallel regions in OpenMP are considered **shared**. This means that all threads within a team have access to the same memory location for that variable.[2]

Example:

C++

```
int counter = 0;
```

```
#pragma omp parallel

{

    counter++; // All threads access and modify the same
'counter' variable

}
```

In this example, counter is a shared variable. If multiple
threads increment it without proper synchronization,
you'll likely encounter a race condition, leading to an
incorrect result.

Private Variables: Isolated within Threads

To avoid race conditions and ensure data integrity,
OpenMP provides the private clause. When you declare
a variable as private within a parallel region, each thread
receives its own unique copy of that variable.
Modifications made to a private variable by one thread
do not affect the private copies in other threads.[3]

Example:

C++

```
#pragma omp parallel private(my_local_var)
```

```
{

    int my_local_var = 0; // Each thread has its own private
'my_local_var'

    my_local_var++;

}
```

Here, my_local_var is private. Each thread has its own copy, so they can modify it independently without interference.[4]

Data-Sharing Attribute Clauses

OpenMP provides several clauses to control data scope:[5]

- shared(list): Explicitly declares a list of variables as shared.
- private(list): Explicitly declares a list of variables as private.[6]
- firstprivate(list): Similar to private, but each private copy is initialized with the value of the original variable before entering the parallel region.
- lastprivate(list): Similar to private, but the value of the original variable is updated with the value from the last thread to complete the parallel region.

- default(shared | none): Specifies the default data scope for variables that are not explicitly listed in other clauses. default(none) forces you to declare the scope of every variable, which can help prevent accidental data sharing.

Choosing the Right Scope

Choosing the appropriate data scope is crucial for writing correct and efficient parallel programs. Here are some guidelines:

- **Shared:** Use for data that needs to be accessed by all threads and is read-only, or when you have mechanisms to synchronize access (e.g., critical sections, atomic operations).
- **Private:** Use for variables that are modified within the parallel region and should be isolated within each thread.
- firstprivate: Use when you need to initialize private variables with values from outside the parallel region.
- lastprivate: Use when you need to preserve the final value of a private variable after the parallel region.[7]

Example with firstprivate:

C++

```
int initial_value = 10;


#pragma omp parallel firstprivate(initial_value)

{

   int my_var = initial_value;  // Each thread's 'my_var'
starts with 10

  // ... calculations using my_var ...

}
```

By understanding the concepts of shared and private variables and utilizing the data-sharing attribute clauses effectively, you can control data scope in your OpenMP programs, prevent race conditions, and ensure the correctness and efficiency of your parallel code.

Critical Sections and Atomic Operations (Protecting shared data)

In concurrent programming, multiple threads often need to access and modify shared data. However, unsynchronized access to shared resources can lead to race conditions and data corruption. To prevent these issues, OpenMP provides mechanisms like critical sections and atomic operations, which allow you to protect shared data and ensure that only one thread accesses it at a time.

Critical Sections: Exclusive Access

A **critical section** is a block of code that must be executed by only one thread at a time. OpenMP provides the #pragma omp critical directive to define critical sections.

Syntax:

```
C++

#pragma omp critical [(name)]

{

  // Code to be executed by only one thread at a time

}
```

The optional (name) allows you to give a name to the critical section, which can be useful for organizing and debugging your code.

Example:

C++

```cpp
int counter = 0;


#pragma omp parallel
{
  #pragma omp critical
  {
      counter++; // Only one thread can increment the counter at a time
  }
}
```

In this example, the #pragma omp critical directive ensures that only one thread can enter the critical section and increment the counter variable at a time. Other threads will wait until the critical section is unlocked before they can enter and modify the shared variable.

Atomic Operations: Fine-grained Synchronization

For simple operations like incrementing a counter or updating a flag, **atomic operations** provide a more fine-grained synchronization mechanism. OpenMP provides the #pragma omp atomic directive to specify that a particular memory location should be updated atomically.

Syntax:

C++

```
#pragma omp atomic

expression;
```

Example:

C++

```
int counter = 0;


#pragma omp parallel

{

  #pragma omp atomic

    counter++; // Atomic increment, no need for a critical section

}
```

In this case, the #pragma omp atomic directive ensures that the counter++ operation is performed atomically, preventing race conditions without the need for a full critical section.

Supported Atomic Operations

OpenMP supports a limited set of atomic operations, including:

- ++ and -- (increment and decrement)
- +=, -=, *=, /=, &=, |=, ^= (arithmetic and bitwise assignments)

Choosing Between Critical Sections and Atomic Operations

- **Critical sections:** More general-purpose, can protect multiple lines of code.
- **Atomic operations:** More efficient for simple operations on single variables, but limited in scope.

If you only need to protect a single, simple operation, atomic operations are generally preferred due to their lower overhead. For more complex scenarios or when you need to protect multiple lines of code, critical sections provide the necessary flexibility.

Important Notes:

- **Deadlocks:** Be careful when using critical sections to avoid deadlocks, which can occur when threads hold locks on multiple critical sections in a conflicting order.
- **Performance:** Excessive use of critical sections can lead to contention and hinder performance. Strive for a balance between protecting shared data and allowing for parallel execution.

By understanding and applying critical sections and atomic operations effectively, you can safeguard shared data in your OpenMP programs, prevent race conditions, and ensure the correctness of your parallel code.

Synchronization Constructs (barrier, single, master)

In parallel programming, it's often necessary to coordinate the actions of multiple threads. OpenMP provides several synchronization constructs that allow you to control the flow of execution and ensure that threads cooperate correctly. Let's explore three essential synchronization constructs: barrier, single, and master.

1. barrier: Synchronizing All Threads

The #pragma omp barrier directive creates a synchronization point within a parallel region. When a thread reaches a barrier, it waits until all other threads in the team have also reached the barrier. Once all threads have arrived, they are released and can continue execution.

Example:

C++

```
#pragma omp parallel
{
    // ... some code executed by all threads ...


    #pragma omp barrier // All threads wait here


    // ... code that should be executed only after all threads
reach the barrier ...

}
```

In this example, the barrier ensures that all threads complete the first part of the code before any thread proceeds to the second part. This can be useful for ensuring that all threads have reached a consistent state before proceeding with further computations.

2. single: Executing Code Once

The #pragma omp single directive specifies that a block of code should be executed by only one thread in the team. Other threads will skip that block and continue execution.

Example:

C++

```cpp
#pragma omp parallel
{
  #pragma omp single
  {
    std::cout << "This will be printed only once by one thread." << std::endl;

    // ... initialization or setup code that needs to be done only once ...

  }
```

```
// ... code executed by all threads ...

}
```

This can be useful for tasks like initializing shared resources, printing output, or performing operations that only need to be done once.

3. master: Code for the Master Thread

The #pragma omp master directive specifies that a block of code should be executed only by the **master thread** (the thread with ID 0). Other threads will skip that block.

Example:

C++

```cpp
#pragma omp parallel
{
  #pragma omp master
  {
    std::cout << "This will be printed only by the master thread." << std::endl;
    // ... code specific to the master thread ...
```

```
}
```

```
// ... code executed by all threads ...

}
```

This can be useful for tasks that are specific to the master thread, such as coordinating the work of other threads or performing I/O operations.

Key Differences

- barrier: All threads wait.
- single: One thread executes, others skip.
- master: Specifically the master thread (thread 0) executes, others skip.

Choosing the Right Construct

The choice of synchronization construct depends on your specific needs:

- Use barrier when you need to synchronize all threads at a specific point.
- Use single when a block of code needs to be executed only once by any thread.
- Use master when a block of code needs to be executed only by the master thread.

By understanding and applying these synchronization constructs, you can effectively coordinate the actions of threads in your OpenMP programs, ensuring correct and efficient parallel execution.

Deadlocks and How to Avoid Them (Scenarios and solutions)

Deadlocks are a dreaded scenario in concurrent programming where two or more threads become stuck in a perpetual standstill, each waiting for the other to release a resource it holds. Imagine a traffic jam where cars block each other at an intersection, unable to move forward. Let's explore how deadlocks occur and, more importantly, how to prevent them.

The Four Ingredients of a Deadlock

For a deadlock to occur, four conditions must be present simultaneously:

1. **Mutual Exclusion:** A resource can be held by only one thread at a time.
2. **Hold and Wait:** A thread holding a resource can request additional resources.
3. **No Preemption:** A resource cannot be forcibly taken away from a thread; it must be released voluntarily.

4. **Circular Wait:** A circular chain of threads exists, where each thread holds a resource that the next thread in the chain is waiting for.

Deadlock Scenario: The Dining Philosophers

A classic example is the "Dining Philosophers" problem:

Imagine five philosophers sitting around a circular table with five chopsticks. Each philosopher needs two chopsticks to eat. If each philosopher picks up one chopstick and then waits for the second one, they'll all be stuck waiting indefinitely, creating a deadlock.

OpenMP and Deadlocks

In OpenMP, deadlocks can occur when using critical sections or other synchronization constructs. If threads acquire locks on critical sections in a conflicting order, they can end up waiting for each other to release the locks, leading to a deadlock.

Example:

C++

```cpp
std::mutex mutex1, mutex2;


#pragma omp parallel
```

```
{
#pragma omp critical(mutex1)
{
// ... do some work ...

#pragma omp critical(mutex2)
{
// ... do more work ...
}
}
}
```

If one thread acquires mutex1 and another thread acquires mutex2 simultaneously, they might then block indefinitely trying to acquire the other mutex.

Preventing Deadlocks

There are several strategies to prevent deadlocks:

1. **Break the Circular Wait:**
   - **Resource Ordering:** Establish a strict order in which threads acquire resources.

If all threads request resources in the same order, circular wait cannot occur.

2. **Eliminate Hold and Wait:**
   ○ **Request All Resources at Once:** If a thread needs multiple resources, it should request them all at once. If any resource is unavailable, the thread should release all previously acquired resources and try again later.

3. **Allow Preemption (Less Common):**
   ○ **Forcefully Release Resources:** In some systems, it might be possible to preempt resources from a thread, but this can be complex and lead to inconsistencies.

4. **Avoid Nested Locks:**
   ○ **Restructure Code:** If possible, restructure your code to avoid nested critical sections or locks.

5. **Use Timeouts:**
   ○ **Limit Waiting Time:** When waiting for a resource, set a timeout. If the resource is not acquired within the timeout period, release any held resources and try again later.

Best Practices in OpenMP

- **Minimize Critical Sections:** Use critical sections only when necessary and keep them as short as possible.
- **Consider Atomic Operations:** For simple operations, prefer atomic operations over critical sections.
- **Analyze Data Dependencies:** Carefully analyze data dependencies to avoid situations where threads might block each other.
- **Test Thoroughly:** Test your code with different numbers of threads and varying workloads to identify potential deadlocks.

By understanding the causes of deadlocks and applying these prevention strategies, you can write robust and deadlock-free OpenMP programs.

Code Samples: Examples showing proper and improper data handling.

C++

```cpp
// Improper Data Handling: Race Condition


#include <iostream>

#include <vector>
```

```cpp
#include <omp.h>

int main() {
  std::vector<int> data(100, 0);
  int sum = 0;

  #pragma omp parallel for
  for (int i = 0; i < data.size(); ++i) {
    sum += i; // Race condition on 'sum'
    data[i] = i * 2;
  }

    std::cout << "Sum: " << sum << std::endl; // Likely
incorrect result

  return 0;
}
```

In this example, multiple threads try to update the shared sum variable simultaneously, leading to a race condition. The final value of sum will likely be incorrect.

C++

```cpp
// Proper Data Handling: Reduction

#include <iostream>
#include <vector>
#include <omp.h>

int main() {
  std::vector<int> data(100, 0);
  int sum = 0;

  #pragma omp parallel for reduction(+:sum)
  for (int i = 0; i < data.size(); ++i) {
    sum += i; // Correctly using reduction for 'sum'
    data[i] = i * 2;
```

```cpp
    }


    std::cout << "Sum: " << sum << std::endl; // Correct
result


    return 0;

}
```

Here, the reduction(+:sum) clause ensures that the sum variable is handled correctly. Each thread has a private copy of sum, and the final result is calculated by combining these private copies.

C++

```cpp
// Improper Data Handling: Shared Loop Counter


#include <iostream>
#include <omp.h>


int main() {
```

```cpp
int counter = 0;


#pragma omp parallel

{

  for (int i = 0; i < 10; ++i) {

    counter++; // Race condition on 'counter'

    std::cout << "Thread " << omp_get_thread_num() <<
": " << counter << std::endl;

  }

}


  return 0;

}
```

In this example, the loop counter i is implicitly shared, leading to a race condition when multiple threads try to increment counter.

C++

// Proper Data Handling: Private Loop Counter

```cpp
#include <iostream>

#include <omp.h>


int main() {
  #pragma omp parallel
  {
      int counter = 0; // 'counter' is now private to each
thread
    for (int i = 0; i < 10; ++i) {
      counter++;
      std::cout << "Thread " << omp_get_thread_num() <<
": " << counter << std::endl;
    }
  }


  return 0;
}
```

By moving counter inside the parallel region, it becomes private to each thread, eliminating the race condition.

These examples highlight the importance of careful data handling in OpenMP. By understanding the concepts of shared and private variables, using appropriate data-sharing clauses, and applying synchronization mechanisms when necessary, you can prevent race conditions and ensure the correctness of your parallel code.

Practice Problems: Identifying and fixing data races in code snippets.

C++

```
// Problem 1:


int total = 0;


#pragma omp parallel for
for (int i = 0; i < 1000; ++i) {
  total += i;
}
```

Identify the issue:

- Multiple threads try to update the shared variable total simultaneously, leading to a race condition.

Fix:

C++

```
int total = 0;
```

```
#pragma omp parallel for reduction(+:total)
for (int i = 0; i < 1000; ++i) {
    total += i;
}
```

- The reduction(+:total) clause ensures that each thread has a private copy of total, and the final result is calculated correctly by combining these copies.

C++

```
// Problem 2:
```

```cpp
std::vector<int> data(100, 0);


#pragma omp parallel for
for (int i = 0; i < data.size(); ++i) {
  int temp = data[i] * 2;
  data[i] = temp;
  // ... other code that might use 'temp' ...
}
```

Identify the issue:

- While there's no direct data race here, the variable temp might be unintentionally shared between threads if the "... other code that might use 'temp' ..." section accesses or modifies temp.

Fix:

C++

```cpp
std::vector<int> data(100, 0);
```

```cpp
#pragma omp parallel for
for (int i = 0; i < data.size(); ++i) {

    int temp = data[i] * 2; // 'temp' is now private to each thread

    data[i] = temp;

    // ... other code that might use 'temp' ...

}
```

- Declaring temp inside the loop makes it private to each thread, preventing potential conflicts.

C++

```cpp
// Problem 3:

bool found = false;

int target = 50;


#pragma omp parallel for
for (int i = 0; i < 1000; ++i) {
```

```cpp
        if (array[i] == target) {

            found = true;

        }

}
```

Identify the issue:

- Multiple threads might try to update the shared found variable simultaneously, leading to a race condition.

Fix:

C++

```cpp
bool found = false;
int target = 50;


#pragma omp parallel for
for (int i = 0; i < 1000; ++i) {

    if (array[i] == target) {

        #pragma omp critical
```

```
    {

    found = true;

    }

    break; // Exit the loop once the target is found

  }

}
```

- A critical section protects the update of found.
  The break statement ensures that the loop
  terminates once the target is found by any thread.

These exercises help you develop the skills to identify
and resolve data races in OpenMP code. Remember to
analyze shared variables, consider potential conflicts
between threads, and use appropriate synchronization
mechanisms to protect shared data and ensure correct
results.

Part III: Advanced OpenMP and Applications

Chapter 6: Tasks and Data Flow

Task-Based Parallelism with OpenMP
(Introducing the task directive)

While OpenMP's for directive excels at parallelizing regular loops, many applications involve irregular or dynamic patterns of parallelism that don't fit neatly into the loop model. This is where **task-based parallelism** comes into play, and OpenMP provides the task directive to express and manage such parallelism effectively.

The task Directive: Creating Units of Work

The task directive allows you to define independent units of work, called **tasks**, that can be executed concurrently by threads in a parallel region. These tasks can be generated dynamically during program execution, enabling flexible and adaptive parallelism.

Syntax:

C++

```
#pragma omp task [clauses]
{
  // Code to be executed as a task
```

```
}
```

When a thread encounters a task directive, it can choose to:

- **Execute the task immediately:** The encountering thread executes the task's code.
- **Defer the task:** The task is added to a pool of tasks, and another thread can pick it up and execute it later.

This flexibility allows OpenMP to dynamically distribute tasks among threads, adapting to the workload and available resources.

Example: Recursive Fibonacci Calculation

C++

```cpp
int fibonacci(int n) {
  if (n <= 1) {
    return n;
  } else {
    int x, y;
    #pragma omp task shared(x)
```

```
x = fibonacci(n - 1);

#pragma omp task shared(y)

y = fibonacci(n - 2);

#pragma omp taskwait

return x + y;

}

}
```

In this example, the fibonacci function creates tasks for the recursive calls. This allows the subproblems to be computed concurrently, potentially speeding up the calculation. The taskwait directive ensures that the parent task waits for its child tasks to complete before proceeding.

Benefits of Task-Based Parallelism

- **Flexibility:** Handles irregular and dynamic parallelism effectively.
- **Adaptability:** OpenMP can dynamically schedule tasks based on workload and available resources.

- **Expressiveness:** Allows you to express parallelism in a more natural way for certain types of algorithms.
- **Efficiency:** Can lead to better performance for applications with complex dependencies or varying workloads.

Key Concepts

- **Task pool:** OpenMP maintains a pool of tasks that can be executed by threads.
- **Task dependencies:** You can specify dependencies between tasks using clauses like depend.
- **Task scheduling:** OpenMP runtime handles the scheduling and execution of tasks.

When to Use Tasks

Task-based parallelism is particularly well-suited for:

- **Recursive algorithms:** Divide-and-conquer algorithms like quicksort or mergesort.
- **Dynamic workloads:** Situations where the number of tasks or their dependencies are not known in advance.
- **Irregular parallelism:** Applications with complex or unpredictable patterns of parallelism.

By understanding and applying the task directive and related concepts, you can leverage task-based parallelism in OpenMP to write more efficient and expressive parallel programs for a wider range of applications.

Dependencies and Task Scheduling

When working with tasks in OpenMP, it's essential to understand how to manage dependencies between tasks and how OpenMP schedules these tasks for execution. This orchestration ensures that tasks are executed in the correct order and that parallelism is exploited effectively.

Task Dependencies: Establishing Order

In many cases, tasks are not entirely independent; they might require results from other tasks before they can begin. OpenMP provides the depend clause within the task directive to express these dependencies.

depend **Clause:**

- depend(in: variable_list): The task depends on the listed variables being **read** by other tasks. The task will not start until all the dependencies are satisfied (i.e., the variables are written to by the tasks they depend on).
- depend(out: variable_list): The task **writes** to the listed variables, and other tasks might depend on these values. The task will not start until any

potentially conflicting tasks that write to the same variables have completed.

- depend(inout: variable_list): The task both reads and writes to the listed variables. This combines the behavior of in and out dependencies.

Example:

C++

```cpp
#pragma omp parallel
{
  #pragma omp task depend(out: a)
  {
    // Calculate the value of 'a'
  }


  #pragma omp task depend(in: a) depend(out: b)
  {
    // Use the value of 'a' to calculate 'b'
  }
```

```
#pragma omp task depend(in: b)

{

  // Use the value of 'b'

  }

}
```

In this example, the second task depends on the first task to calculate a, and the third task depends on the second task to calculate b. OpenMP ensures that the tasks are executed in the correct order to satisfy these dependencies.

Task Scheduling: Dynamic and Decentralized

OpenMP employs a dynamic and decentralized approach to task scheduling. When a thread encounters a task directive, it can choose to execute the task immediately or defer it to the task pool. Other threads can then steal tasks from the pool and execute them. This allows for efficient load balancing and adaptation to varying workloads.

Factors Influencing Scheduling:

- **Task dependencies:** OpenMP prioritizes tasks whose dependencies have been satisfied.

- **Thread availability:** Idle threads actively look for tasks to execute.
- **Data locality:** OpenMP tries to schedule tasks on threads that have access to the required data, minimizing data movement.
- **Implementation details:** The specific scheduling algorithm can vary between OpenMP implementations.

taskyield **Directive:**

The taskyield directive provides a hint to the OpenMP runtime that the current thread is willing to yield execution to another thread that might be ready to execute a task. This can be useful in situations where a thread is waiting for a long-running task to complete.

Example:

C++

```
#pragma omp task
{
  // ... long-running task ...
}
```

```
#pragma omp taskyield // Allow other threads to
execute tasks
```

```
// ... code that can be executed concurrently ...
```

Benefits of Dynamic Scheduling:

- **Load balancing:** Distributes tasks evenly among threads.
- **Adaptability:** Adjusts to varying workloads and resource availability.
- **Efficiency:** Minimizes idle time and maximizes resource utilization.

By understanding task dependencies and how OpenMP schedules tasks, you can effectively orchestrate the flow of tasks in your parallel programs, ensuring correct execution and maximizing performance.

Data Dependencies and depend Clause

In the realm of task-based parallelism, where tasks reign supreme as independent units of work, it's crucial to recognize that these tasks often don't exist in isolation. They frequently rely on data produced or consumed by other tasks, creating intricate relationships that must be carefully managed. This is where the concept of **data dependencies** and the power of the depend clause come into play.

Data Dependencies: The Ties that Bind

A data dependency arises when one task relies on data produced by another task. This creates an inherent order of execution: the dependent task cannot begin its work until the task it depends on has finished producing the necessary data.

Types of Data Dependencies

- **Read-after-write (RAW):** A task needs to **read** data that another task **writes**. This is the most common type of dependency.
- **Write-after-read (WAR):** A task needs to **write** to a location that another task **reads** from. This dependency ensures that the read happens before the write.
- **Write-after-write (WAW):** A task needs to **write** to a location that another task also **writes** to. This dependency ensures that writes happen in the correct order to avoid data corruption.

The depend Clause: Expressing Dependencies

OpenMP provides the depend clause within the task directive to explicitly specify data dependencies between tasks. This clause allows you to define the direction of the dependency (in, out, or inout) and the variables involved.

Syntax:

C++

#**pragma** omp task depend(type: variable_list)

- **type:** in, out, or inout, specifying the dependency type.
- **variable_list:** A comma-separated list of variables involved in the dependency.

Example: Producer-Consumer Pattern

C++

#**include** <queue>

std::queue<int> data_queue;

#**pragma** omp parallel
{

```
#pragma omp task depend(out: data_queue)

{

    // Producer task: Generate data and add it to the queue

    data_queue.push(10);

    data_queue.push(20);

}


#pragma omp task depend(in: data_queue)

{

    // Consumer task: Retrieve data from the queue and
process it

    int data = data_queue.front();

    data_queue.pop();

    // ... process data ...

}

}
```

In this example, the consumer task depends on the producer task to generate data and add it to the queue.

The depend(in: data_queue) clause ensures that the consumer task waits until the producer task has added data to the queue.

Benefits of the depend Clause

- **Correctness:** Ensures that tasks are executed in the correct order to avoid data races and maintain data integrity.
- **Efficiency:** Allows OpenMP to optimize task scheduling by taking dependencies into account.
- **Expressiveness:** Provides a clear and concise way to express data dependencies between tasks.

Key Considerations

- **Accuracy:** Specify dependencies accurately to avoid introducing unnecessary synchronization or creating deadlocks.
- **Granularity:** Consider the granularity of dependencies. Fine-grained dependencies might increase overhead, while coarse-grained dependencies might limit parallelism.
- **Performance:** Analyze the impact of dependencies on performance. Excessive dependencies can hinder parallelism and reduce efficiency.

By understanding data dependencies and utilizing the depend clause effectively, you can ensure the correct execution of tasks in your OpenMP programs, maintain data integrity, and optimize performance.

Code Samples: Examples of task-based parallelism for recursive algorithms and irregular computations.

C++

```cpp
// Example 1: Recursive Quicksort

#include <vector>
#include <omp.h>

void quicksort(std::vector<int>& arr, int low, int high) {
  if (low < high) {
    int pi = partition(arr, low, high);

    #pragma omp task
    quicksort(arr, low, pi - 1);
```

```cpp
    #pragma omp task
    quicksort(arr, pi + 1, high);
  }
}


int main() {
  std::vector<int> data = {10, 7, 8, 9, 1, 5};

  #pragma omp parallel
  {
    #pragma omp single
    quicksort(data, 0, data.size() - 1);
  }

  // ... print sorted data ...
  return 0;
}
```

In this example, quicksort recursively divides the array into subarrays. The #pragma omp task directives create tasks for sorting the subarrays, enabling parallel execution of the recursive calls. The #pragma omp single ensures that the initial call to quicksort is only executed once.

C++

```cpp
// Example 2: Merge Sort


#include <vector>
#include <omp.h>


void merge_sort(std::vector<int>& arr, int left, int right)
{
  if (left < right) {
    int mid = left + (right - left) / 2;


    #pragma omp task
    { merge_sort(arr, left, mid); }
```

```cpp
    #pragma omp task
    { merge_sort(arr, mid + 1, right); }


    #pragma omp taskwait

    merge(arr, left, mid, right); // Assuming you have a
'merge' function

  }
}


int main() {
  std::vector<int> data = {12, 11, 13, 5, 6, 7};


  #pragma omp parallel
  {
  #pragma omp single nowait
  { merge_sort(data, 0, data.size() - 1); }
  }
```

```cpp
// ... print sorted data ...

return 0;

}
```

This example demonstrates task-based parallelism for merge sort. Tasks are created for sorting the left and right halves of the array. The #pragma omp taskwait ensures that the merge operation happens only after both halves are sorted.

C++

```cpp
// Example 3:  Irregular Computation (Flood Fill)


#include <vector>

#include <omp.h>


void flood_fill(std::vector<std::vector<int>>& image, int sr, int sc, int newColor) {

  int oldColor = image[sr][sc];

  if (oldColor == newColor) return;
```

```cpp
    image[sr][sc] = newColor;


    #pragma omp task
    if (sr + 1 < image.size())    flood_fill(image, sr + 1, sc,
    newColor);

    #pragma omp task
    if (sr >= 1)                  flood_fill(image, sr - 1, sc,
    newColor);

    #pragma omp task
    if (sc + 1 < image[0].size()) flood_fill(image, sr, sc + 1,
    newColor);

    #pragma omp task
    if (sc >= 1)                  flood_fill(image, sr, sc - 1,
    newColor);
}


int main() {
    std::vector<std::vector<int>> image = {
        {1, 1, 1},
```

```
  {1, 1, 0},

  {1, 0, 1}

};


#pragma omp parallel

{

  #pragma omp single

  flood_fill(image, 1, 1, 2);

}


// ... print modified image ...

return 0;

}
```

This example shows a simplified flood fill algorithm. Tasks are created for exploring neighboring pixels, enabling parallel execution of the fill operation in different directions. This demonstrates how tasks can be used for irregular computations where the flow of execution depends on the data.

These examples illustrate the versatility of task-based parallelism in OpenMP. By creating tasks for independent or loosely coupled parts of your computation, you can effectively parallelize recursive algorithms and irregular computations, leading to improved performance and more expressive code.

Practice Problems: Implementing parallel algorithms using tasks.

These practice problems will challenge you to implement various parallel algorithms using OpenMP tasks, allowing you to explore the power and flexibility of task-based parallelism:

1. Parallel Merge Sort:

- Implement the merge sort algorithm using OpenMP tasks.
- Create tasks for recursively sorting the left and right halves of the input array.
- Use taskwait to ensure that the merge operation happens only after both halves are sorted.
- Experiment with different input sizes and observe the performance improvement compared to a sequential implementation.

2. Parallel N-Queens:

- Implement the N-Queens problem using OpenMP tasks.
- Create tasks for exploring different possible positions for the queens on the chessboard.
- Use task dependencies (depend clause) to ensure that placements in the same row or diagonal are not explored concurrently.
- Compare the performance with a sequential solution, especially for larger values of N.

3. Parallel Tree Traversal:

- Implement a parallel tree traversal algorithm (e.g., depth-first search or breadth-first search) using OpenMP tasks.
- Create tasks for exploring different branches of the tree concurrently.
- Use task dependencies to ensure that nodes are visited in the correct order.
- Test with different tree structures and sizes to evaluate the performance.

4. Parallel Graph Algorithms:

- Implement a parallel graph algorithm, such as:
    - Breadth-first search
    - Depth-first search
    - Shortest path algorithms (e.g., Dijkstra's algorithm)

- Minimum spanning tree algorithms (e.g., Prim's algorithm)
- Use OpenMP tasks to explore different parts of the graph concurrently.
- Apply task dependencies to manage data dependencies between tasks.
- Evaluate the performance with different graph sizes and structures.

5. Parallel Fractal Generation:

- Implement a parallel fractal generation algorithm (e.g., Mandelbrot set or Julia set) using OpenMP tasks.
- Create tasks for calculating different regions of the fractal image concurrently.
- Use task dependencies to ensure that calculations that depend on previous results are executed in the correct order.
- Visualize the generated fractal and compare the performance with a sequential implementation.

Challenge Problem: Parallel Game AI

- Implement a parallel game AI for a simple game (e.g., tic-tac-toe or Connect Four) using OpenMP tasks.
- Create tasks for exploring different possible moves and evaluating their outcomes.

- Use task dependencies to manage the search tree and ensure that moves are evaluated in the correct order.
- Play against the AI and observe its performance.

These practice problems encourage you to apply task-based parallelism to a variety of algorithms. By implementing these algorithms using OpenMP tasks, you will gain valuable experience in managing task dependencies, orchestrating task execution, and optimizing performance. Remember to analyze the results and compare them with sequential implementations to understand the benefits of task-based parallelism.

Chapter 7: Memory Model and Performance Optimization

The OpenMP Memory Model (Consistency, Flushing, Data races)

Understanding the OpenMP memory model is crucial for writing correct and efficient parallel programs. It defines how threads interact with shared memory and provides mechanisms to ensure consistency and avoid data races.

Shared Memory and Temporary Views

OpenMP employs a shared-memory model where all threads within a parallel region have access to the same global memory. However, each thread also has its own **temporary view of memory**. This temporary view acts as a cache, allowing threads to work with data locally and reduce communication overhead.

Consistency and Flushing

The temporary view of a thread may not always be consistent with the global memory. To ensure consistency, OpenMP provides the **flush** operation. A flush operation makes a thread's temporary view consistent with the global memory, ensuring that changes made by one thread are visible to other threads.

Implicit Flushes

OpenMP performs implicit flushes at certain points, such as:

- Entering or exiting a parallel region
- Entering or exiting a critical section
- At a barrier

Explicit Flushes

You can also explicitly flush specific variables or all shared variables using the #pragma omp flush directive.

Example:

C++

```
#pragma omp parallel
{
  // ... some code ...


  #pragma omp flush(x, y) // Flush variables x and y


  // ... more code ...
}
```

Flush Sets

Each flush operation has an associated **flush set**, which is the set of variables that are guaranteed to be consistent with global memory after the flush. Implicit flushes typically have a flush set that includes all shared variables, while explicit flushes can have a more limited flush set.

Data Races: The Perils of Inconsistency

A **data race** occurs when multiple threads access the same memory location concurrently, and at least one of the accesses is a write[1] operation, without proper synchronization. Data races can lead to unpredictable and incorrect results due to inconsistencies between temporary views and global memory.

Example:

C++

```
int counter = 0;


#pragma omp parallel
{
```

```
counter++; // Potential data race

}
```

In this example, multiple threads increment the counter variable without synchronization. This can result in lost updates because threads might read the same value of counter from their temporary views, increment it, and write it back, overwriting each other's changes.

Preventing Data Races

To prevent data races, use synchronization mechanisms like:

- **Critical sections:** Ensure that only one thread accesses the shared data at a time.
- **Atomic operations:** Provide fine-grained synchronization for simple operations.
- **Reductions:** Safely combine results from parallel loops.

Memory Model and Performance

The OpenMP memory model provides a balance between performance and consistency. Temporary views allow threads to work with data locally, reducing communication overhead. However, it's essential to use synchronization mechanisms and flushes appropriately to ensure data consistency and avoid data races, which can lead to incorrect results and undermine performance.

Key Takeaways

- OpenMP uses a shared-memory model with temporary views for each thread.
- Flushes ensure consistency between temporary views and global memory.
- Data races occur when shared data is accessed concurrently without synchronization.
- Synchronization mechanisms and flushes are essential for preventing data races and ensuring correctness.

By understanding the OpenMP memory model, you can write efficient and correct parallel programs that leverage the power of shared memory while avoiding the pitfalls of data races and inconsistencies.

Performance Considerations (Load balancing, False sharing, Overhead)

While OpenMP makes it relatively easy to parallelize your code, achieving optimal performance requires careful consideration of several factors. Let's explore some key performance considerations that can significantly impact the efficiency of your OpenMP programs.

1. Load Balancing: Distributing Work Evenly

Load balancing refers to distributing the workload evenly among threads to minimize idle time and maximize resource utilization. If some threads are overloaded while others are idle, it creates a bottleneck and hinders overall performance.

Factors Affecting Load Balancing:

- **Loop scheduling:** Choose the appropriate loop scheduling strategy (static, dynamic, guided) based on the workload distribution of your loops.
- **Task dependencies:** Be mindful of task dependencies, as they can create imbalances if some tasks have to wait for others to complete.
- **Data locality:** Try to schedule tasks on threads that have access to the required data to minimize data movement and communication overhead.

Techniques for Improving Load Balancing:

- **Dynamic scheduling:** Use dynamic or guided scheduling for loops with varying workloads.
- **Task chunking:** Divide large tasks into smaller chunks that can be distributed more evenly.
- **Work stealing:** Allow idle threads to steal tasks from busy threads.

2. False Sharing: The Cache Line Conundrum

False sharing occurs when multiple threads access different variables that happen to reside on the same cache line. Even though the threads are working on independent data, the cache line bounces back and forth between their caches, creating unnecessary communication and slowing down the program.

Cache Lines:

Modern processors use cache lines, which are small blocks of memory, to store frequently accessed data. When a thread modifies a variable in a cache line, the entire cache line needs to be synchronized with other threads that might have a copy of that cache line.

Mitigating False Sharing:

- **Data padding:** Insert padding (dummy variables) between variables that are likely to be accessed by different threads. This ensures that they fall on different cache lines.
- **Data alignment:** Align data structures to cache line boundaries to prevent them from spanning multiple cache lines.
- **Data restructuring:** Reorganize data structures to group variables that are accessed by the same thread together.

3. Overhead: The Cost of Parallelism

Parallelism comes with some overhead, including:

- **Thread creation and management:** Creating and managing threads takes time and resources.
- **Synchronization:** Synchronization mechanisms like critical sections and barriers can introduce delays if threads have to wait for each other.
- **Data communication:** Moving data between threads or between memory and caches can incur overhead.

Minimizing Overhead:

- **Reduce thread creation:** Reuse threads instead of creating new ones for each parallel region.
- **Minimize synchronization:** Use synchronization only when necessary and keep critical sections as short as possible.
- **Optimize data locality:** Structure your data and code to minimize data movement and communication.

Finding the Balance

Optimizing performance often involves finding the right balance between parallelism and overhead. Over-parallelization can lead to increased overhead that outweighs the benefits of parallelism. It's essential to profile your code, identify performance bottlenecks, and focus on parallelizing the most computationally intensive parts.

By considering these performance factors, you can write OpenMP programs that efficiently utilize multicore processors and achieve significant speedups.

Profiling and Tuning OpenMP Applications (Tools and techniques)

Writing parallel programs with OpenMP is just the first step. To truly unleash the power of multicore processors, you need to **profile** your applications to identify performance bottlenecks and then **tune** your code to optimize for speed and efficiency. This section explores the tools and techniques that can help you achieve peak performance.

Profiling: Unveiling the Bottlenecks

Profiling is the process of analyzing your program's execution to identify where it spends its time and resources. This analysis reveals performance hotspots, such as sections of code that take a long time to execute, regions with excessive synchronization overhead, or areas with poor load balancing.

Profiling Tools

Several profiling tools are available for OpenMP applications, including:

- **gprof:** A standard Unix profiling tool that provides function-level profiling data.
- **Valgrind (with Callgrind):** A powerful memory debugging and profiling tool that can also analyze cache misses and branch prediction.
- **Intel VTune Amplifier:** A comprehensive performance analysis tool that provides detailed insights into CPU utilization, memory access patterns, and threading behavior.
- **TAU (Tuning and Analysis Utilities):** A portable profiling and tracing toolkit for parallel applications.
- **OmpP:** A lightweight profiler specifically designed for OpenMP programs.

Profiling Techniques

- **Timing measurements:** Measure the execution time of different sections of your code to identify hotspots.
- **Event-based profiling:** Track specific events, such as thread creation, synchronization, and data transfers.
- **Statistical profiling:** Sample the program's execution at regular intervals to get a statistical overview of where time is spent.

Tuning: Fine-tuning for Speed

Once you've identified performance bottlenecks through profiling, you can apply various tuning techniques to optimize your code:

- **Loop optimization:**
    - Choose the appropriate loop scheduling strategy (static, dynamic, guided).
    - Adjust chunk sizes to optimize for load balancing.
    - Consider loop unrolling or vectorization to improve instruction-level parallelism.
- **Data optimization:**
    - Minimize data sharing and contention.
    - Use appropriate data-sharing clauses (private, shared, reduction).
    - Pad or align data to avoid false sharing.
- **Synchronization optimization:**
    - Reduce the use of critical sections.
    - Prefer atomic operations for simple operations.
    - Consider using fine-grained locks or lock-free data structures.
- **Task optimization:**
    - Adjust task granularity to balance parallelism and overhead.
    - Use task dependencies effectively to ensure correct execution.

- Consider using taskyield to allow threads to yield to other tasks.
- **Algorithm optimization:**
  - Choose algorithms that are well-suited for parallel execution.
  - Consider using divide-and-conquer or pipeline parallelism.

Iterative Optimization

Performance optimization is an iterative process. Profile your code, identify bottlenecks, apply tuning techniques, and then profile again to measure the impact of your changes. Repeat this process until you achieve satisfactory performance.

Tips for Effective Tuning

- **Focus on the hotspots:** Prioritize optimizing the most time-consuming parts of your code.
- **Measure the impact:** Always measure the performance impact of your changes to ensure they are actually improving things.
- **Consider trade-offs:** Be aware of trade-offs between different optimization techniques. For example, reducing synchronization might increase the risk of data races.

- **Don't over-optimize:** Avoid premature optimization. Focus on correctness and readability first, then optimize for performance.

By combining profiling tools and tuning techniques, you can unlock the full potential of OpenMP and achieve significant performance improvements in your parallel applications.

Best Practices: Writing efficient and scalable OpenMP code.

To truly harness the power of OpenMP and create high-performance parallel applications, it's essential to follow best practices that promote efficiency, scalability, and maintainability. This section distills key recommendations to guide you in writing robust and optimized OpenMP code.

1. Start with a Correct Serial Version

Before introducing parallelism, ensure your serial code is correct and efficient. Parallelism amplifies existing issues, so starting with a solid foundation is crucial. Profile your serial code to identify potential bottlenecks and optimize them before parallelizing.

2. Focus on the Hotspots

Don't parallelize everything! Identify the most computationally intensive parts of your code (the hotspots) through profiling and focus your parallelization efforts there. Amdahl's Law reminds us that the speedup from parallelization is limited by the portion of the code that cannot be parallelized.

3. Minimize Data Sharing and Contention

Shared data is a common source of contention and performance bottlenecks in parallel programs. Strive to:

- **Reduce shared data:** Use the private clause to give each thread its own copy of variables whenever possible.
- **Use local variables:** Declare variables within parallel regions to make them private by default.
- **Protect shared data:** Use synchronization mechanisms (critical sections, atomic operations) only when necessary to protect shared data.
- **Consider thread-local storage:** For data that needs to be unique to each thread throughout its lifetime, explore thread-local storage (TLS).

4. Choose the Right Synchronization

Select the most appropriate synchronization mechanism based on your needs:

- **Critical sections:** For protecting blocks of code.

- **Atomic operations:** For simple operations on single variables.
- **Reductions:** For combining results from parallel loops.
- **Barriers:** For synchronizing all threads at a specific point.

5. Optimize Loop Scheduling

Choose the loop scheduling strategy (static, dynamic, guided) that best suits the workload distribution of your loops. Experiment with different chunk sizes to fine-tune load balancing.

6. Avoid False Sharing

Pad or align data structures to prevent false sharing, where multiple threads modify different variables that happen to reside on the same cache line.

7. Minimize Thread Creation Overhead

Creating threads can be expensive. If possible, reuse threads by creating them once and using them for multiple parallel regions.

8. Use Tasks for Irregular Parallelism

For recursive algorithms, dynamic workloads, or irregular patterns of parallelism, leverage OpenMP tasks to express and manage parallelism effectively.

9. Test and Profile Thoroughly

Test your parallel code with different numbers of threads and varying workloads to identify potential issues like race conditions or deadlocks. Use profiling tools to analyze performance and identify areas for optimization.

10. Write Maintainable Code

- **Keep it simple:** Avoid overly complex parallel structures that are difficult to understand and maintain.
- **Use meaningful variable names:** Choose names that clearly indicate the purpose and scope of variables.
- **Add comments:** Explain the logic behind your parallelization choices.

By adhering to these best practices, you can write efficient, scalable, and maintainable OpenMP code that effectively utilizes the power of multicore processors and delivers high performance.

Code Samples: Optimized and unoptimized code versions with performance comparisons.

C++

// Unoptimized: False Sharing

```cpp
#include <vector>
#include <omp.h>

struct Data {
  int value1;
  int value2;
};

int main() {
  std::vector<Data> data(1000);

  #pragma omp parallel for
  for (int i = 0; i < data.size(); ++i) {
```

```cpp
    data[i].value1 = i * 2; // Thread 0 might access this

    // ... some unrelated code ...

    data[i].value2 = i * 3; // Thread 1 might access this

}


    return 0;

}
```

Problem: value1 and value2 are likely to be on the same cache line. If different threads access them, it can cause false sharing.

C++

```cpp
// Optimized: Padding to Avoid False Sharing


#include <vector>
#include <omp.h>


struct Data {
```

```cpp
    int value1;

    char padding[56]; // Add padding to ensure value2 is on
a different cache line

    int value2;

};


int main() {

    std::vector<Data> data(1000);


    #pragma omp parallel for
    for (int i = 0; i < data.size(); ++i) {
      data[i].value1 = i * 2;
      // ... some unrelated code ...
      data[i].value2 = i * 3;
    }


    return 0;

}
```

Improvement: Padding ensures value1 and value2 are on different cache lines, reducing false sharing.

C++

```cpp
// Unoptimized: Excessive Critical Sections

#include <vector>
#include <omp.h>

int main() {
  std::vector<int> data(1000);
  int sum = 0;

  #pragma omp parallel for
  for (int i = 0; i < data.size(); ++i) {
    #pragma omp critical
    {
      sum += data[i]; // Critical section for every iteration!
```

```
    }

  }


  return 0;

}
```

Problem: A critical section for every iteration creates significant overhead.

C++

// Optimized: Reduction

```cpp
#include <vector>
#include <omp.h>

int main() {
  std::vector<int> data(1000);
  int sum = 0;
```

```cpp
#pragma omp parallel for reduction(+:sum)

for (int i = 0; i < data.size(); ++i) {

    sum += data[i]; // Efficient reduction

}


    return 0;

}
```

Improvement: Using a reduction eliminates the need for critical sections, significantly reducing overhead.

C++

```cpp
// Unoptimized: Unnecessary Thread Creation


#include <iostream>

#include <omp.h>


void process_data(int i) {

    // ... some time-consuming operation ...
```

```cpp
}

int main() {

  for (int i = 0; i < 100; ++i) {

    #pragma omp parallel // Creating threads for each iteration!

    {

      process_data(i);

    }

  }


  return 0;

}
```

Problem: Creating threads for each iteration is very inefficient.

C++

// Optimized: Thread Reuse

```cpp
#include <iostream>
#include <omp.h>

void process_data(int i) {
    // ... some time-consuming operation ...
}

int main() {
    #pragma omp parallel
    {
        for (int i = 0; i < 100; ++i) {
            process_data(i); // Threads are reused for all iterations
        }
    }

    return 0;
```

}

Improvement: Threads are created once and reused for all iterations, reducing overhead.

These examples demonstrate how seemingly small changes can have a significant impact on performance. By applying optimization techniques and avoiding common pitfalls, you can write OpenMP code that efficiently utilizes multicore processors and delivers excellent results.

Practice Problems: Optimizing existing OpenMP programs.

C++

```cpp
// Problem 1: Optimize this code for load balancing


#include <vector>
#include <omp.h>


int main() {
```

```cpp
std::vector<int> data(1000);

#pragma omp parallel for schedule(static)
for (int i = 0; i < data.size(); ++i) {
  if (i % 2 == 0) {
    // Simulate a long computation for even iterations
    for (int j = 0; j < 1000000; ++j) {}
  }
  data[i] = i * 2;
}

return 0;
}
```

Hints:

- The workload is unevenly distributed due to the longer computation for even iterations.
- Consider using dynamic or guided scheduling to improve load balancing.

- Experiment with different chunk sizes.

C++

```cpp
// Problem 2: Optimize this code to avoid false sharing

#include <vector>
#include <omp.h>

struct Data {
  int value1;
  int value2;
};

int main() {
  std::vector<Data> data(1000);

  #pragma omp parallel for
  for (int i = 0; i < data.size(); ++i) {
    data[i].value1 = i * 2; // Thread 0 might access this
```

```cpp
    data[i].value2 = i * 3; // Thread 1 might access this
}


  return 0;

}
```

Hints:

- value1 and value2 are likely on the same cache line, potentially causing false sharing.
- Add padding to the Data struct to ensure value1 and value2 are on different cache lines.

C++

```cpp
// Problem 3: Optimize this code to reduce
synchronization overhead


#include <vector>
#include <omp.h>


int main() {
```

```cpp
std::vector<int> data(1000);
int sum = 0;


#pragma omp parallel
{
  #pragma omp for
  for (int i = 0; i < data.size(); ++i) {
    #pragma omp critical
    {
      sum += data[i];
    }
  }
}


return 0;
}
```

Hints:

- The critical section for every iteration creates significant overhead.
- Consider using a reduction to efficiently calculate the sum without critical sections.

C++

```cpp
// Problem 4: Optimize this code to reduce thread creation overhead


#include <iostream>
#include <omp.h>


void process_data(int i) {
    // ... some time-consuming operation ...
}


int main() {
    for (int i = 0; i < 100; ++i) {
        #pragma omp parallel
        {
```

```
      process_data(i);

    }

  }


  return 0;

}
```

Hints:

- Creating threads for each iteration is inefficient.
- Move the #pragma omp parallel directive outside the loop to reuse threads.

These practice problems encourage you to apply your knowledge of OpenMP performance considerations to optimize existing code. By analyzing the code, identifying potential bottlenecks, and applying appropriate optimization techniques, you can significantly improve the efficiency and scalability of your parallel programs.

Chapter 8: Real-World Applications

Case Study 1: Image Processing (Parallel image filtering or edge detection)

Image processing is a computationally intensive field that often involves applying operations to large images, making it an ideal candidate for parallelization.[1] In this case study, we'll explore how to use OpenMP to accelerate image filtering or edge detection, demonstrating the practical application of the concepts we've learned.

Understanding Image Filtering and Edge Detection

- **Image Filtering:** Involves applying a filter (a small matrix) to each pixel in an image.[2] This filter modifies the pixel's value based on the values of its neighboring pixels. Common filters include blurring, sharpening, and noise reduction filters.[3]
- **Edge Detection:** Aims to identify the boundaries of objects in an image by detecting sharp changes in intensity or color.[4] Popular edge detection algorithms include Sobel, Prewitt, and Canny edge detectors.[5]

Parallelization Strategy

The core idea is to divide the image into smaller regions and process these regions in parallel using OpenMP. Each thread will be responsible for applying the filter or edge detection algorithm to its assigned region.

Steps:

1. **Load the Image:** Use an image processing library (e.g., OpenCV, ImageMagick) to load the image into memory.
2. **Divide the Image:** Divide the image into smaller rectangular regions or tiles. The number of regions should ideally be a multiple of the number of available threads.
3. **Parallelize the Processing:** Use OpenMP's parallel for directive to distribute the regions among threads. Each thread will apply the filter or edge detection algorithm to its assigned region.
4. **Combine the Results:** If necessary, combine the processed regions to form the final output image.

Code Example (Parallel Image Filtering with a Box Blur):

C++

```cpp
#include <opencv2/opencv.hpp>

#include <omp.h>
```

```cpp
int main() {

  cv::Mat image = cv::imread("input.jpg");

  cv::Mat blurred_image = cv::Mat::zeros(image.size(),
image.type());


  int kernel_size = 5; // Size of the box blur kernel


#pragma omp parallel for
  for (int i = kernel_size / 2; i < image.rows - kernel_size
/ 2; ++i) {

    for (int j = kernel_size / 2; j < image.cols - kernel_size
/ 2; ++j) {

      cv::Scalar sum = cv::Scalar::all(0);

      for (int k = -kernel_size / 2; k <= kernel_size / 2;
++k) {

        for (int l = -kernel_size / 2; l <= kernel_size / 2;
++l) {

          sum += image.at<cv::Vec3b>(i + k, j + l);

        }
```

```
        }

                blurred_image.at<cv::Vec3b>(i,  j)  =  sum  /
(kernel_size * kernel_size);

    }

}


cv::imwrite("blurred_output.jpg", blurred_image);

return 0;

}
```

Explanation:

- This code uses OpenCV to load and manipulate the image.
- The outer for loop iterates over the rows of the image, and the inner for loop iterates over the columns.
- The #pragma omp parallel for directive parallelizes the outer loop, distributing rows among threads.
- Each thread calculates the average color of the neighboring pixels within the kernel size and applies it to the current pixel.

Performance Considerations

- **Load balancing:** If the image has regions with varying complexity (e.g., some areas have more edges than others), consider using dynamic scheduling to improve load balancing.
- **False sharing:** Ensure that neighboring pixels processed by different threads do not fall on the same cache line to avoid false sharing.
- **Synchronization:** If the filter or edge detection algorithm requires accessing shared data (e.g., accumulating results), use appropriate synchronization mechanisms.

Extending the Example

You can adapt this example to implement other image processing operations, such as:

- **Different filters:** Gaussian blur, median filter, sharpening filter.
- **Edge detection algorithms:** Sobel, Prewitt, Canny.
- **Image transformations:** Rotation, scaling, warping.

Conclusion

This case study demonstrates how OpenMP can be applied to accelerate image processing tasks. By dividing the image into smaller regions and processing them in parallel, you can significantly reduce the execution time and improve the efficiency of your image processing applications.

Case Study 2: Scientific Simulation (N-body problem, Monte Carlo methods)

Scientific simulations often involve complex calculations on large datasets, making them prime candidates for parallelization. In this case study, we'll delve into two common types of scientific simulations—the N-body problem and Monte Carlo methods—and explore how OpenMP can be used to accelerate their execution.

1. The N-body Problem: Simulating Gravitational Interactions

The N-body problem involves simulating the motion of a system of particles under the influence of gravitational forces.[1] This problem has applications in astrophysics (simulating galaxies and star clusters), molecular dynamics (studying the behavior of molecules), and fluid dynamics (modeling the flow of liquids and gases).

Parallelization Strategy

The key to parallelizing the N-body problem is to divide the computation of forces between particles among multiple threads. Each thread can be responsible for calculating the forces exerted on a subset of particles by all other particles in the system.

Steps:

1. **Initialize Particles:** Define the initial positions, velocities, and masses of the particles.
2. **Calculate Forces:** Use OpenMP's parallel for directive to distribute the force calculations among threads. Each thread calculates the force exerted on its assigned particles by all other particles.
3. **Update Positions and Velocities:** Once the forces are calculated, update the positions and velocities of the particles based on the forces and a chosen time step.
4. **Repeat:** Repeat steps 2 and 3 for the desired number of time steps.

Code Example (Simplified N-body Simulation):

```cpp
C++

#include <vector>
#include <omp.h>
```

```cpp
#include <cmath>

struct Particle {
  double x, y, z; // Position
  double vx, vy, vz; // Velocity
  double mass;
};


void calculate_forces(std::vector<Particle>& particles) {
  #pragma omp parallel for
  for (int i = 0; i < particles.size(); ++i) {
   for (int j = 0; j < particles.size(); ++j) {
    if (i != j) {
        // Calculate gravitational force between particles i
and j
      // ... (omitted for brevity) ...
        // Update the velocity of particle i based on the
force
      }
```

```
        }

    }

}

int main() {

    std::vector<Particle> particles = { /* ... initialize
particles ... */ };


    for (int step = 0; step < num_steps; ++step) {

    calculate_forces(particles);

    // ... update positions of particles ...

    }


    return 0;

}
```

Performance Considerations:

- **Load balancing:** If the distribution of particles is uneven (e.g., denser in some regions), consider using dynamic scheduling to improve load balancing.

- **Data locality:** Try to store particles that interact frequently close together in memory to improve cache utilization.
- **Synchronization:** If the force calculation or position updates require accessing shared data, use appropriate synchronization mechanisms.

2. Monte Carlo Methods: Harnessing Randomness

Monte Carlo methods use random sampling to solve problems that might be deterministic in principle.[2] They have applications in various fields, including physics (simulating particle interactions), finance (option pricing), and engineering (reliability analysis).[3]

Parallelization Strategy

The key to parallelizing Monte Carlo methods is to perform multiple independent simulations concurrently. Each thread can be responsible for running a separate simulation with a different random seed.

Steps:

1. **Generate Random Numbers:** Use a thread-safe random number generator to generate random numbers for each thread.

2. **Run Simulations:** Use OpenMP's parallel for directive to distribute the simulations among threads. Each thread performs its simulation using its own set of random numbers.
3. **Combine Results:** Combine the results from all simulations to obtain the final result (e.g., calculate the average or estimate a probability).

Code Example (Estimating Pi using Monte Carlo):

C++

```cpp
#include <omp.h>

#include <random>


int main() {
  long long num_points = 1000000;

  long long num_inside_circle = 0;


  #pragma omp parallel reduction(+:num_inside_circle)

  {

    std::random_device rd;

    std::mt19937 gen(rd());
```

```cpp
    std::uniform_real_distribution<> dis(0.0, 1.0);

    #pragma omp for
    for (long long i = 0; i < num_points; ++i) {
      double x = dis(gen);
      double y = dis(gen);
      if (x * x + y * y <= 1.0) {
        num_inside_circle++;
      }
    }
  }

    double pi_estimate = 4.0 * num_inside_circle /
num_points;

  return 0;
}
```

Performance Considerations:

- **Load balancing:** Ensure that each thread performs a similar amount of work.
- **Random number generation:** Use a thread-safe random number generator to avoid race conditions and ensure independent simulations.
- **Synchronization:** If the simulations require accessing shared data, use appropriate synchronization mechanisms.

Conclusion

This case study highlights how OpenMP can be applied to accelerate scientific simulations. By parallelizing the computation of forces in the N-body problem or running multiple independent simulations in Monte Carlo methods, you can significantly reduce the execution time and enable more complex and accurate simulations.

Case Study 3: Financial Modeling (Option pricing, Portfolio optimization)

Financial modeling often involves computationally intensive tasks that can benefit greatly from parallelization.[1] In this case study, we'll explore how OpenMP can be applied to accelerate two common financial modeling problems: option pricing and portfolio optimization.

1. Option Pricing: Valuing Derivatives

Options are financial derivatives that give the holder the right, but not the obligation, to buy or sell an underlying asset at a specified price[2] (strike price) on or before a certain date (expiration date).[3] Pricing options accurately is crucial for risk management and investment decision-making.[4]

Parallelization Strategy

Many option pricing models, particularly those involving Monte Carlo simulations, are inherently parallelizable.[5] The core idea is to run multiple independent simulations concurrently, each with a different random seed.

Steps:

1. **Generate Random Paths:** Use a thread-safe random number generator to generate multiple paths for the underlying asset's price. Each path represents a possible evolution of the asset's price over time.
2. **Calculate Payoffs:** For each path, calculate the payoff of the option at expiration.
3. **Discount Payoffs:** Discount the payoffs back to the present value using a risk-free interest rate.[6]
4. **Average Payoffs:** Average the discounted payoffs across all paths to estimate the option's price.[7]

Code Example (European Call Option Pricing with Monte Carlo):

C++

```
#include <omp.h>

#include <cmath>

#include <random>


double european_call_option_price(double S, double K, double r, double sigma, double T, int num_paths) {
  double sum_payoffs = 0.0;


  #pragma omp parallel reduction(+:sum_payoffs)
  {
    std::random_device rd;
    std::mt19937 gen(rd());
    std::normal_distribution<> normal(0.0, 1.0);


    #pragma omp for
```

```cpp
    for (int i = 0; i < num_paths; ++i) {

        double ST = S * exp((r - 0.5 * sigma * sigma) * T +
sigma * sqrt(T) * normal(gen));

        sum_payoffs += std::max(ST - K, 0.0);

    }

}


    return exp(-r * T) * sum_payoffs / num_paths;

}


int main() {

  // ... set parameters S, K, r, sigma, T, num_paths ...


    double price = european_call_option_price(S, K, r,
sigma, T, num_paths);


    return 0;

}
```

Performance Considerations:

- **Load balancing:** Ensure that each thread simulates a similar number of paths.
- **Random number generation:** Use a thread-safe random number generator to avoid race conditions and ensure independent simulations.
- **Variance reduction techniques:** Explore variance reduction techniques (e.g., antithetic variates, control variates) to improve the accuracy and efficiency of the simulation.[8]

2. Portfolio Optimization: Maximizing Returns, Minimizing Risk

Portfolio optimization involves selecting the optimal combination of assets to invest in, aiming to maximize returns while minimizing risk.[9] This requires solving complex optimization problems, often involving large covariance matrices and constraints.

Parallelization Strategy

Several approaches can be used to parallelize portfolio optimization:

- **Parallel algorithms:** Implement parallel versions of optimization algorithms (e.g., genetic algorithms, simulated annealing) to explore the solution space concurrently.

- **Divide-and-conquer:** Divide the optimization problem into smaller subproblems, solve them in parallel, and then combine the solutions.
- **Parallel linear algebra:** Use parallel linear algebra libraries (e.g., BLAS, LAPACK) to accelerate matrix operations involved in the optimization process.

Code Example (Parallel Portfolio Optimization with a Genetic Algorithm):

C++

```cpp
#include <omp.h>

#include <vector>

// ... other includes for genetic algorithm implementation
...




// ... (omitted for brevity: functions for fitness evaluation,
crossover, mutation, etc.) ...



int main() {

  // ... initialize population, parameters, etc. ...
```

```cpp
for (int generation = 0; generation < num_generations;
++generation) {

  #pragma omp parallel for

  for (int i = 0; i < population_size; ++i) {

    // ... evaluate fitness, perform crossover and mutation
  ...

  }

  // ... select the next generation ...

}


// ... find the best solution ...

return 0;

}
```

Performance Considerations:

- **Load balancing:** Ensure that each thread handles a similar portion of the population or search space.

- **Synchronization:** If the fitness evaluation or genetic operations require accessing shared data, use appropriate synchronization mechanisms.
- **Algorithm choice:** Select an optimization algorithm that is well-suited for parallelization.

Conclusion

This case study demonstrates how OpenMP can be applied to accelerate financial modeling tasks. By parallelizing option pricing simulations or portfolio optimization algorithms, you can significantly reduce the computation time and enable more complex and accurate financial models.

Project Guidelines: Outlines for more extensive projects related to each case study.

These project outlines provide more extensive explorations of the concepts introduced in the case studies, allowing readers to delve deeper and apply their OpenMP skills to more challenging and realistic scenarios.

Project 1: Advanced Image Processing
- **Objective:** Develop a more comprehensive image processing application that incorporates multiple filters and edge detection algorithms.

- **Features:**
  - Implement a variety of filters (e.g., Gaussian blur, median filter, sharpening filter).
  - Implement different edge detection algorithms (e.g., Sobel, Prewitt, Canny).
  - Allow the user to select and combine different filters and edge detectors.
  - Provide options for adjusting parameters (e.g., kernel size, thresholds).
  - Optimize the code for performance using appropriate OpenMP directives and techniques.
- **Possible Extensions:**
  - Implement image segmentation algorithms to identify objects in the image.
  - Implement feature extraction techniques to extract relevant information from the image.
  - Develop a graphical user interface (GUI) for the application.

Project 2: Realistic N-body Simulation

- **Objective:** Create a more realistic N-body simulation that incorporates additional physical phenomena and visualization.
- **Features:**

- Implement more accurate force calculations (e.g., Barnes-Hut algorithm for faster computation).
- Incorporate collision detection and handling.
- Add support for different types of particles (e.g., with varying masses and charges).
- Visualize the simulation using a graphics library (e.g., OpenGL).[1]
- Optimize the code for performance using advanced OpenMP techniques.
- **Possible Extensions:**
  - Implement a user interface for controlling simulation parameters and visualizing results.
  - Add support for external forces (e.g., magnetic fields).
  - Simulate more complex systems (e.g., galaxies with millions of stars).

Project 3: Sophisticated Financial Modeling

- **Objective:** Develop a more sophisticated financial modeling application that includes advanced option pricing models and portfolio optimization techniques.
- **Features:**

- Implement more complex option pricing models (e.g., binomial tree models, finite difference methods).
- Incorporate different risk factors and market dynamics.
- Implement advanced portfolio optimization techniques (e.g., mean-variance optimization, Black-Litterman model).
- Allow the user to define constraints and preferences for portfolio optimization.
- Optimize the code for performance using OpenMP and potentially GPUs.

- **Possible Extensions:**
  - Develop a user interface for inputting data and visualizing results.
  - Integrate with real-time market data feeds.
  - Implement backtesting and risk analysis tools.

General Guidelines for Projects

- **Start with a plan:** Clearly define the project's objectives, features, and scope.
- **Break down the problem:** Divide the project into smaller, manageable tasks.

- **Use version control:** Use a version control system (e.g., Git) to track changes and collaborate effectively.[2]
- **Test thoroughly:** Test the code regularly to ensure correctness and identify potential issues.
- **Profile and optimize:** Use profiling tools to analyze performance and optimize the code for efficiency.
- **Document your code:** Add clear comments and documentation to explain the logic and design choices.

By undertaking these projects, readers will gain valuable experience in applying OpenMP to real-world problems, developing their skills in parallel programming, and building a portfolio of impressive applications.

Chapter 9: Debugging and Troubleshooting

Common OpenMP Errors (Race conditions, Deadlocks, Performance issues)

Debugging parallel programs can be more challenging than debugging serial code due to the non-deterministic nature of thread execution and the complexities of shared memory. This section explores common errors that can arise in OpenMP programs, providing insights into their causes and guidance on how to identify and resolve them.

1. Race Conditions: The Perils of Unprotected Data

Race conditions occur when multiple threads access and modify shared data simultaneously without proper synchronization. This can lead to unpredictable and incorrect results, as the outcome depends on the unpredictable timing of thread execution.

Symptoms:

- Inconsistent results that vary between runs.
- Program crashes or unexpected behavior.
- Values of variables that don't make sense.

Debugging Techniques:

- **Examine shared variables:** Carefully analyze all shared variables and identify any potential for concurrent access without synchronization.
- **Use debugging tools:** Utilize debuggers with OpenMP support to step through the code, examine thread states, and identify race conditions.
- **Insert print statements:** Add print statements to track the values of shared variables and the order of thread execution.
- **Reduce the number of threads:** Running the program with fewer threads can sometimes make race conditions more apparent.

Solutions:

- **Critical sections:** Use #pragma omp critical to protect shared data and ensure exclusive access.
- **Atomic operations:** Use #pragma omp atomic for simple operations on single variables.
- **Reductions:** Use the reduction clause to safely combine results from parallel loops.
- **Proper data scoping:** Use the private, shared, and other data-sharing clauses to control the scope of variables and prevent unintended sharing.

2. Deadlocks: The Unbreakable Embrace

Deadlocks occur when two or more threads become stuck in a circular wait, each holding a resource that another thread needs to proceed. This can bring your program to a grinding halt.

Symptoms:

- Program hangs or freezes indefinitely.
- Threads are blocked and unable to make progress.

Debugging Techniques:

- **Analyze locking patterns:** Carefully examine the order in which threads acquire and release locks (e.g., critical sections). Look for potential circular dependencies.
- **Use debugging tools:** Debuggers can help you visualize thread states and identify deadlocks.
- **Print stack traces:** Print stack traces of threads to see where they are blocked.

Solutions:

- **Consistent locking order:** Establish a consistent order in which threads acquire locks to prevent circular dependencies.
- **Avoid nested locks:** If possible, restructure your code to avoid nested critical sections or locks.
- **Use timeouts:** When waiting for a lock, set a timeout to prevent indefinite blocking.

3. Performance Issues: When Parallelism Doesn't Pay Off

While parallelism can significantly improve performance, it's not always a guaranteed win. Sometimes, parallel code might perform worse than serial code due to various factors.

Symptoms:

- Parallel code runs slower than serial code.
- Performance does not scale as expected with increasing numbers of threads.

Debugging Techniques:

- **Profiling:** Use profiling tools (e.g., gprof, Valgrind, Intel VTune Amplifier) to identify performance bottlenecks.
- **Analyze load balancing:** Ensure that work is distributed evenly among threads. Look for uneven loop iterations or task dependencies that might cause imbalances.
- **Check for false sharing:** Ensure that different threads are not accessing data on the same cache line, leading to false sharing.
- **Minimize overhead:** Reduce thread creation overhead, synchronization overhead, and data communication overhead.

Solutions:

- **Optimize loop scheduling:** Choose the appropriate loop scheduling strategy and chunk size.
- **Improve data locality:** Structure your data and code to minimize data movement and communication.
- **Reduce synchronization:** Use synchronization only when necessary and keep critical sections as short as possible.
- **Avoid over-parallelization:** Don't parallelize everything. Focus on the most computationally intensive parts of your code.

By understanding these common OpenMP errors and applying the debugging techniques and solutions presented, you can effectively troubleshoot your parallel programs and ensure they are correct, efficient, and scalable.

Debugging Tools and Techniques (Debuggers with OpenMP support)

Debugging parallel programs, especially those using OpenMP, requires a specialized set of tools and techniques to tackle the unique challenges that arise from concurrent execution. This section explores essential debugging tools and strategies to help you identify and resolve errors in your OpenMP code.

Debuggers with OpenMP Support

Traditional debuggers often fall short when dealing with parallel programs. Fortunately, several debuggers offer explicit support for OpenMP, providing features tailored to the complexities of multithreaded execution.

1. GDB (GNU Debugger)

GDB, a widely used open-source debugger, provides robust support for debugging OpenMP programs. It allows you to:

- Set breakpoints in parallel regions.
- Step through code thread by thread.
- Examine thread-specific variables.
- Inspect the state of OpenMP constructs (e.g., locks, barriers).

2. LLDB (LLVM Debugger)

LLDB, another powerful open-source debugger, offers similar capabilities to GDB for debugging OpenMP applications. It integrates well with the LLVM compiler infrastructure and provides a modern and extensible debugging experience.

3. Intel Debugger (IDB)

Intel Debugger is a commercial debugger that provides comprehensive support for debugging OpenMP programs on Intel platforms. It offers advanced features for analyzing parallel performance, identifying race conditions, and visualizing thread interactions.

4. TotalView

TotalView is a commercial debugger specifically designed for high-performance computing (HPC) applications, including those using OpenMP. It offers a rich set of features for debugging parallel programs, including support for MPI and CUDA.

Debugging Techniques

Beyond specialized debuggers, several techniques can aid in debugging OpenMP programs:

1. Conditional Breakpoints

Set breakpoints that trigger only under specific conditions, such as when a particular thread reaches a certain line of code or when a shared variable takes on a specific value. This allows you to focus on relevant parts of the execution.

2. Logging and Tracing

Insert print statements or use logging libraries to track the execution flow of different threads, the values of shared variables, and the state of synchronization constructs. However, be mindful that excessive logging can introduce overhead and alter timing, potentially masking race conditions.

3. Data Race Detection Tools

Specialized tools like Helgrind (part of Valgrind) and Intel Inspector can help detect data races by dynamically analyzing memory accesses and identifying potential conflicts between threads.

4. Reduce Non-Determinism

To make debugging more predictable, try to reduce non-determinism in your code. This can be achieved by:

- Setting the number of threads explicitly.
- Using a deterministic loop scheduling strategy (e.g., static).
- Seeding the random number generator with a fixed value.

5. Simplify and Isolate

If you encounter complex errors, try to simplify your code by isolating the problematic section or creating a smaller test case that reproduces the issue. This can make it easier to identify the root cause.

Tips for Effective Debugging

- Start with a correct serial version: Ensure your serial code is correct before introducing parallelism.
- Test with different numbers of threads: Vary the number of threads to expose potential concurrency issues.
- Be patient and methodical: Debugging parallel programs can be challenging. Take a systematic approach and use the available tools and techniques effectively.

By combining these debugging tools and techniques, you can effectively troubleshoot your OpenMP programs, identify and resolve errors, and ensure the correctness and reliability of your parallel code.

Tips for Writing Maintainable OpenMP Code

As your OpenMP projects grow in complexity, maintaining and extending your code becomes crucial. Writing maintainable parallel code requires a mindful approach that prioritizes clarity, organization, and readability, ensuring that your code remains understandable and adaptable over time. Here are some key tips to guide you:

1. Keep it Simple

Avoid overly complex parallel structures or nesting too many OpenMP directives. Break down complex tasks into smaller, more manageable parallel regions. This improves readability and makes it easier to reason about the code's behavior.

2. Use Meaningful Variable Names

Choose descriptive variable names that clearly indicate their purpose and scope (e.g., shared_counter, private_result, thread_local_data). This improves code comprehension and reduces the chance of errors due to confusion about variable usage.

3. Add Comments

Explain the rationale behind your parallelization choices. Document why you chose a specific OpenMP directive, scheduling strategy, or synchronization mechanism. This helps others (and your future self) understand the code's design and intent.

4. Structure Your Code

Organize your code into logical functions and modules. Separate parallel regions from serial code to improve readability and make it easier to identify parallel sections.

5. Use Consistent Formatting

Adopt a consistent code formatting style (e.g., indentation, spacing, braces placement). This enhances readability and makes it easier to spot inconsistencies or errors.

6. Avoid Premature Optimization

Focus on writing correct and readable code first. Optimize for performance only after you have a working and well-structured solution. Premature optimization can lead to complex and less maintainable code.

7. Test Thoroughly

Write comprehensive tests to verify the correctness of your parallel code. Test with different numbers of threads and varying workloads to uncover potential concurrency issues.

8. Use Version Control

Use a version control system (e.g., Git) to track changes, experiment with different approaches, and collaborate effectively with others.

9. Stay Updated

Keep abreast of the latest OpenMP standards and best practices. New versions of OpenMP often introduce features or optimizations that can improve your code's efficiency and maintainability.

10. Seek Feedback

Have other developers review your code. Fresh perspectives can often identify areas for improvement in terms of clarity, efficiency, or maintainability.

Example: Well-Commented Code

C++

```
#pragma omp parallel for schedule(dynamic, 10) // Use dynamic scheduling for load balancing

for (int i = 0; i < data.size(); ++i) {

  // This loop processes data elements independently, so no synchronization is needed.

  process_data(data[i]);
```

}

By following these tips, you can create OpenMP code that is not only efficient but also easy to understand, modify, and extend. This investment in maintainability will pay off in the long run as your projects evolve and grow.

Chapter 10: Beyond the Basics

Advanced OpenMP Features (SIMD directives, Nested parallelism)

This chapter delves into more advanced OpenMP features that can further enhance the performance and expressiveness of your parallel programs. We'll explore SIMD directives for exploiting vectorization and nested parallelism for creating hierarchical parallel structures.

1. SIMD Directives: Harnessing Vectorization

Modern processors often include Single Instruction, Multiple Data (SIMD) units that can perform the same operation on multiple data elements simultaneously. OpenMP provides SIMD directives to guide the compiler in generating code that utilizes these SIMD capabilities, leading to significant performance gains for certain types of computations.

#pragma omp simd

The #pragma omp simd directive instructs the compiler to vectorize the following loop, if possible. This means that the loop iterations will be executed in groups, with each group processed concurrently by the SIMD unit.

Example:

C++

```cpp
#pragma omp simd

for (int i = 0; i < n; ++i) {

  a[i] = b[i] + c[i]; // Vectorizable operation

}
```

SIMD Clauses

Several clauses can be used with #pragma omp simd to control vectorization:

- aligned(list): Specifies that the listed arrays are aligned to a specific boundary, which can improve vectorization efficiency.
- linear(list:step): Indicates that the listed arrays are accessed linearly with a specified step.
- reduction(operator:variable): Performs a reduction operation on the specified variable across the SIMD lanes.

Performance Considerations

- Data alignment: Proper data alignment is crucial for efficient vectorization.

- Loop structure: Loops with simple, independent iterations are more likely to be vectorized effectively.
- Data dependencies: Avoid data dependencies between iterations within a SIMD chunk.

2. Nested Parallelism: Hierarchical Parallelism

Nested parallelism allows you to create parallel regions within other parallel regions, forming a hierarchical structure of threads. This can be useful for expressing parallelism at multiple levels of granularity.

Enabling Nested Parallelism

Nested parallelism is typically disabled by default. You can enable it using:

- The OMP_NESTED environment variable.
- The omp_set_nested() function.

Example:

C++

```
#pragma omp parallel

{

  #pragma omp parallel for // Nested parallel region

  for (int i = 0; i < n; ++i) {
```

```
    // ... code executed by threads in the inner parallel
region ...

    }

}
```

Performance Considerations

- Overhead: Nested parallelism can introduce additional overhead due to thread creation and management.
- Scalability: The effectiveness of nested parallelism depends on the hardware and the nature of the computation.
- Complexity: Nested parallelism can make the code more complex and harder to reason about.

When to Use Nested Parallelism

Consider nested parallelism when:

- You have multiple levels of parallelism in your algorithm.
- The outer level of parallelism has limited scalability (e.g., due to a small number of iterations).
- The inner level of parallelism can effectively utilize the available cores.

Combining SIMD and Nested Parallelism

You can combine SIMD directives with nested parallelism to achieve both thread-level and SIMD-level parallelism. This can be particularly effective for computationally intensive loops where both approaches can contribute to performance gains.

Example:

C++

```cpp
#pragma omp parallel for
for (int i = 0; i < n; ++i) {
  #pragma omp simd
  for (int j = 0; j < m; ++j) {
    // ... vectorizable code ...
  }
}
```

By understanding and applying these advanced OpenMP features, you can further optimize your parallel programs and achieve even greater performance and scalability. However, always consider the potential overhead and complexity associated with these features and use them judiciously.

Combining OpenMP with Other Concurrency Models (e.g., MPI)

While OpenMP excels at shared-memory parallelism within a single node, many high-performance computing applications require scaling beyond a single node to utilize clusters or supercomputers with distributed memory. This is where combining OpenMP with other concurrency models, such as MPI (Message Passing Interface), becomes essential.

MPI: The King of Distributed Memory

MPI is a standard for message-passing between processes running on different nodes. It allows processes to communicate and synchronize with each other by sending and receiving messages, enabling parallel execution across a distributed system.

Hybrid Parallelism: OpenMP + MPI

A hybrid approach that combines OpenMP and MPI can leverage the strengths of both models:

- **OpenMP for shared-memory parallelism within nodes:** Exploit the shared memory within each node using OpenMP for fine-grained parallelism.

- **MPI for distributed-memory parallelism across nodes:** Use MPI to coordinate the work of different nodes and communicate data between them.

This hybrid approach is often referred to as **MPI+OpenMP** or **hybrid programming**.

Benefits of Hybrid Parallelism

- **Scalability:** Scale your applications to larger systems by utilizing multiple nodes.
- **Efficiency:** Combine the efficiency of OpenMP for shared-memory parallelism with the scalability of MPI for distributed memory.
- **Flexibility:** Adapt to different hardware architectures and configurations.
- **Performance portability:** Write code that can perform well on a variety of systems, from multicore desktops to large supercomputers.

Implementation Considerations

- **Data decomposition:** Carefully decompose your data and computations to distribute them effectively across nodes and threads.

- **Communication:** Minimize communication overhead between nodes by using efficient MPI communication patterns.
- **Synchronization:** Coordinate the work of threads within nodes using OpenMP synchronization constructs and coordinate the work of processes across nodes using MPI synchronization.
- **Load balancing:** Ensure that work is distributed evenly across both nodes and threads.

Example: Hybrid Matrix Multiplication

Imagine multiplying two large matrices, A and B, to produce matrix C. You could use a hybrid approach where:

1. **MPI for data distribution:** Divide matrices A and B into blocks and distribute these blocks among different MPI processes.
2. **OpenMP for parallel computation:** Within each MPI process, use OpenMP to parallelize the multiplication of the assigned blocks using multiple threads.
3. **MPI for result gathering:** Use MPI to gather the results from all processes and assemble the final matrix C.

Code Snippet:

```cpp
C++

#include <mpi.h>

#include <omp.h>


// ... (omitted for brevity: matrix data structures and
functions) ...


int main(int argc, char** argv) {

  MPI_Init(&argc, &argv);

  // ... get rank and size ...


  // ... distribute matrix blocks ...


  #pragma omp parallel for
  for (int i = 0; i < local_rows; ++i) {

    for (int j = 0; j < local_cols; ++j) {

      // ... calculate C[i][j] using OpenMP threads ...

    }
```

```
}


// ... gather results using MPI ...


MPI_Finalize();

return 0;

}
```

Challenges and Considerations

- **Complexity:** Hybrid programming can be more complex than using a single concurrency model.
- **Debugging:** Debugging hybrid programs can be challenging due to the interaction between OpenMP and MPI.
- **Performance tuning:** Optimizing hybrid programs requires careful consideration of both shared-memory and distributed-memory performance factors.

Beyond MPI

OpenMP can also be combined with other concurrency models, such as CUDA or OpenCL for GPU acceleration, or Pthreads for low-level thread management. The choice of concurrency model depends on the specific needs of your application and the target hardware.

By combining OpenMP with other concurrency models, you can create highly scalable and efficient parallel applications that can tackle complex problems on a variety of high-performance computing platforms.

Future Directions of OpenMP

OpenMP continues to evolve to meet the challenges and opportunities of modern parallel computing. The OpenMP Architecture Review Board (ARB) actively works on improving the standard, adding new features, and enhancing existing ones to keep pace with advancements in hardware and software. Here are some key future directions for OpenMP:

1. Enhanced Task-Based Parallelism

Task-based parallelism is becoming increasingly important in OpenMP, and future versions are likely to see further enhancements in this area. This might include:

- **Improved task dependencies:** More expressive ways to specify dependencies between tasks, including potentially data-flow-based dependencies.

- **Task priorities:** Allowing programmers to assign priorities to tasks to influence scheduling decisions.
- **Task groups:** Grouping tasks together to manage and synchronize them collectively.
- **Enhanced cancellation:** More robust mechanisms for canceling tasks and handling cancellations.

2. Accelerator Support

As accelerators like GPUs and FPGAs become more prevalent, OpenMP is actively working on improving support for offloading computations to these devices. This includes:

- **More flexible offloading:** Easier ways to specify which code should be offloaded and how data should be transferred.
- **Unified memory:** Support for unified memory models that simplify data management between host and device.
- **Improved performance modeling:** Better tools for predicting and analyzing the performance of offloaded code.

3. Improved Error Handling

OpenMP is placing greater emphasis on error handling and resilience. This might involve:

- **More informative error messages:** Providing more detailed and helpful error messages to aid in debugging.
- **Exception handling:** Better integration with exception handling mechanisms to gracefully handle errors in parallel regions.
- **Fault tolerance:** Mechanisms for detecting and recovering from failures in parallel computations.

4. Language Features and Integration

OpenMP is continuously evolving to better integrate with modern C++ features and standards. This includes:

- **C++ attribute syntax:** Adopting C++ attribute syntax for OpenMP directives to improve code readability and compatibility with other C++ tools.
- **Lambda expressions:** Better support for using lambda expressions within OpenMP constructs.
- **Concurrency features:** Closer integration with C++ concurrency features like std::thread and std::future.

5. Performance and Productivity

OpenMP is committed to improving both performance and productivity. This involves:

- **New optimizations:** Developing new compiler optimizations and runtime libraries to maximize performance.
- **Simplified programming:** Making OpenMP easier to use and learn, with more intuitive directives and clearer semantics.
- **Better tools:** Providing better tools for profiling, debugging, and tuning OpenMP applications.

Beyond Version 5.2

OpenMP 5.2, released in November 2021, brought significant improvements to the specification and addressed many inconsistencies. Future versions, starting with OpenMP 6.0, are expected to focus on more substantial features and enhancements, building upon the foundation laid by previous versions.

Staying Informed

To stay up-to-date on the latest developments in OpenMP, you can:

- Visit the official OpenMP website: https://www.openmp.org/
- Follow the OpenMP ARB on social media.
- Attend OpenMP conferences and workshops.

- Participate in OpenMP forums and mailing lists.

By staying informed about the future directions of OpenMP, you can ensure that your parallel programming skills remain relevant and that you can leverage the latest advancements to create high-performance and efficient applications.

Appendices

OpenMP Directive Summary (Quick reference)

This appendix provides a concise summary of commonly used OpenMP directives, serving as a quick reference for developers writing parallel programs with OpenMP.

1. Parallel Regions

- #pragma omp parallel [clauses]
    - Creates a parallel region where the enclosed code is executed by multiple threads.
    - Clauses: private, shared, firstprivate, lastprivate, default, num_threads, if, reduction

2. Work-Sharing Constructs

- #pragma omp for [clauses]
    - Distributes loop iterations among threads in a parallel region.
    - Clauses: schedule, collapse, ordered, nowait, private, lastprivate, reduction
- #pragma omp sections [clauses]
    - Divides a block of code into sections, with each thread executing a different section.

- Clauses: nowait, private, firstprivate, lastprivate
- #pragma omp single [clauses]
  - Specifies that the enclosed code should be executed by only one thread.
  - Clauses: nowait, private, firstprivate
- #pragma omp task [clauses]
  - Creates a task that can be executed concurrently by a thread.
  - Clauses: untied, if, final, depend, priority
- #pragma omp taskwait
  - Suspends the current task until all child tasks have completed.

3. Synchronization Constructs

- #pragma omp critical [(name)]
  - Defines a critical section that can be executed by only one thread at a time.
- #pragma omp atomic
  - Ensures that a simple update operation is performed atomically.
- #pragma omp barrier
  - Creates a synchronization point where all threads wait until all other threads have reached the barrier.
- #pragma omp master
  - Specifies that the enclosed code should be executed only by the master thread.

4. Data Environment Directives

- #pragma omp threadprivate(variable_list)
  - Declares that the listed variables should have thread-local storage.

5. Runtime Library Routines

- omp_set_num_threads(int num_threads)
  - Sets the number of threads to use for subsequent parallel regions.
- omp_get_num_threads()
  - Returns the number of threads in the current team.
- omp_get_thread_num()
  - Returns the thread ID of the current thread.
- omp_get_wtime()
  - Returns the current wall clock time.

6. SIMD Directives

- #pragma omp simd [clauses]
  - Instructs the compiler to vectorize the following loop.
  - Clauses: aligned, linear, reduction

7. Nested Parallelism

- OMP_NESTED environment variable
  - Enables or disables nested parallelism.

- omp_set_nested(int nested)
  - ○ Enables or disables nested parallelism.

Note: This is not an exhaustive list of all OpenMP directives and clauses. For a complete reference, consult the official OpenMP specification.

Glossary of Terms

This glossary provides definitions for common terms used throughout the book, helping readers understand the language and concepts of concurrent programming with OpenMP.

A

- **Amdahl's Law:** A formula that gives the theoretical speedup of a program as a function of the portion of the program that can be parallelized and the number of processors.
- **API (Application Programming Interface):** A set of definitions, protocols, and tools for building software applications. OpenMP is an API for parallel programming.
- **Atomic Operation:** An operation that is indivisible and uninterruptible, ensuring that it is executed as a single, complete unit.
- **Attribute Clause:** In OpenMP, clauses that specify properties of variables or directives (e.g., private, shared, reduction).

B

- **Barrier:** A synchronization construct where all threads wait until all other threads have reached the barrier before proceeding.

C

- **Cache Line:** A small block of memory that is transferred between main memory and the processor's cache.
- **Concurrency:** The ability of a program to execute multiple tasks seemingly at the same time.
- **Contention:** When multiple threads compete for access to the same resource (e.g., shared data, a lock).
- **Critical Section:** A block of code that must be executed by only one thread at a time to avoid race conditions.

D

- **Data Dependency:** When one task relies on data produced by another task.
- **Data Race:** When multiple threads access the same memory location concurrently, and at least one access is a write, without proper synchronization.
- **Deadlock:** A situation where two or more threads are blocked indefinitely, each waiting for the other to release a resource.
- **Directive:** In OpenMP, a special comment that instructs the compiler to generate parallel code (e.g., #pragma omp parallel).

- **Distributed Memory:** A memory architecture where each processor has its own private memory, and data must be explicitly communicated between processors.

F

- **False Sharing:** When multiple threads access different variables that happen to reside on the same cache line, leading to unnecessary cache invalidations and performance degradation.
- **Flush:** An operation that makes a thread's temporary view of memory consistent with the global memory.

L

- **Load Balancing:** Distributing the workload evenly among threads to minimize idle time and maximize resource utilization.

M

- **Master Thread:** The thread with ID 0 in an OpenMP parallel region.
- **Memory Model:** A set of rules that define how threads interact with shared memory and how data is made consistent between threads.
- **MPI (Message Passing Interface):** A standard for message-passing between processes running

on different nodes in a distributed memory system.

- **Mutual Exclusion:** When only one thread can access a resource (e.g., shared data, a lock) at a time.

N

- **Nested Parallelism:** Creating parallel regions within other parallel regions, forming a hierarchical structure of threads.

O

- **OpenMP (Open Multi-Processing):** An API for shared-memory parallel programming in C, C++, and Fortran.
- **Overhead:** The extra time and resources required to manage parallelism, including thread creation, synchronization, and data communication.

P

- **Parallelism:** The simultaneous execution of multiple tasks on different processors or cores.
- **Parallel Region:** A block of code that is executed by multiple threads concurrently.
- **Preemption:** Forcibly taking away a resource (e.g., a lock) from a thread.
- **Private Variable:** A variable that has a separate copy for each thread in a parallel region.

R

- **Race Condition:** When the behavior of a program depends on the unpredictable timing of events, such as the order in which threads execute.
- **Reduction:** An operation that combines values from multiple threads into a single result (e.g., sum, maximum).

S

- **Scalability:** The ability of a program to perform well as the number of processors or cores increases.
- **Shared Memory:** A memory architecture where all processors have access to the same global memory.
- **Shared Variable:** A variable that is accessible to all threads in a parallel region.
- **SIMD (Single Instruction, Multiple Data):** A type of processor architecture that can perform the same operation on multiple data elements simultaneously.
- **Synchronization:** Coordinating the actions of multiple threads to ensure correct execution and avoid data races.

T

- **Task:** An independent unit of work in OpenMP that can be executed concurrently by a thread.
- **Task Dependency:** A relationship between tasks where one task depends on the completion of another task.
- **Thread:** A lightweight unit of execution within a process.
- **Thread Safety:** The property of code or data structures that can be safely accessed by multiple threads concurrently.
- **Throughput:** The amount of work that can be done in a given amount of time.

W

- **Work-Sharing:** Distributing the workload among threads in a parallel region (e.g., using #pragma omp for).

Further Reading and Resources

This appendix provides a curated list of resources to deepen your understanding of OpenMP and explore more advanced topics in parallel programming.

Books

- **"Using OpenMP: Portable Shared Memory Parallel Programming"** by Barbara Chapman, Gabriele Jost, and Ruud van der Pas: A comprehensive[1] guide to OpenMP, covering both basic and advanced concepts with detailed explanations and examples.
- **"Parallel Programming in OpenMP"** by Rohit Chandra, Ramesh Menon, Leo Dagum, David Kohr, Dror Maydan, and Jeff McDonald: A classic text that provides a thorough introduction to OpenMP and its applications in scientific and engineering computing.
- **"An Introduction to Parallel Programming"** by Peter Pacheco: A broader introduction to parallel programming that covers various models, including OpenMP, MPI, and CUDA.

Online Resources

- **OpenMP Official Website:** https://www.openmp.org/ The official website for

OpenMP, containing the latest specifications, documentation, and resources.

- **LLNL OpenMP Tutorial:** https://computing.llnl.gov/tutorials/openMP/ A comprehensive tutorial from Lawrence Livermore National Laboratory that covers various aspects of OpenMP with clear explanations and examples.
- **OpenMP.org Resources:** https://www.openmp.org/resources/ A collection of resources from the OpenMP community, including tutorials, presentations, and articles.
- **Stack Overflow:** https://stackoverflow.com/questions/tagged/openmp A valuable resource for finding answers to specific OpenMP questions and getting help from the community.

Tutorials and Articles

- **"A Hands-on Introduction to OpenMP"** by Tim Mattson: https://www.openmp.org/wp-content/uploads/omp-hands-on-SC08.pdf A concise and practical introduction to OpenMP with hands-on exercises.
- **"OpenMP Tutorial"** by Blaise Barney: [invalid URL removed] A comprehensive tutorial that covers various OpenMP features and provides examples.

Tools

- **Intel VTune Amplifier:** https://software.intel.com/content/www/us/en/develop/tools/oneapi/components/vtune-profiler.html[2] A performance analysis tool that provides detailed insights into OpenMP program behavior.
- **Valgrind (with Callgrind):** https://valgrind.org/ A powerful memory debugging and profiling tool that can also analyze OpenMP programs.
- **TAU (Tuning and Analysis Utilities):** http://tau.uoregon.edu/ A portable profiling and tracing toolkit for parallel applications, including OpenMP.

Communities and Forums

- **OpenMP ARB Forum:** https://forum.openmp.org/ The official forum for OpenMP discussions and questions.
- **OpenMP Mailing Lists:** Mailing lists for OpenMP users and developers.

By exploring these resources, you can further enhance your knowledge of OpenMP, stay up-to-date with the latest developments, and connect with the vibrant community of parallel programmers.